THE ISLANDS SERIES

THE UISTS AND BARRA

THE ISLANDS SERIES

Achill
Alderney
†The Aran Islands
The Isle of Arran
The Island of Bute
*Canary Islands: Fuerteventura
*Cape Breton Island
*Corsica
*Cyprus
†Dominica
*The Falkland Islands
†Gotland
*Grand Bahama
†Harris and Lewis
†The Isle of Mull
Lundy
The Maltese Islands
†Mauritius
†Orkney
*Puerto Rico
†Rhodes
St Kilda and Other Hebridean Islands
*The Seychelles
†Shetland
*Singapore
Skye
*The Solomon Islands
*Tasmania
*Vancouver Island

in preparation
Bermuda
Fiji
Guernsey
St Helena
Tobago

---

* Published in the United States by Stackpole
† Published in the United States by David & Charles
  The series is distributed in Australia by Wren

THE UISTS AND BARRA

by FRANCIS THOMPSON

DAVID & CHARLES

NEWTON ABBOT LONDON NORTH POMFRET (VT) VANCOUVER

ISBN 0 7153 6676 9

Library of Congress Catalog Card Number 74-81056

/

Gu luchd nan Eilean

Set in 11 on 13 point Baskerville and printed in
Great Britain by Latimer Trend & Company
Ltd Plymouth for David & Charles (Holdings)
Limited South Devon House Newton Abbot
Devon

Published in the United States of America by
David & Charles Inc North Pomfret Vermont
05053 USA

Published in Canada by Douglas David &
Charles Limited   3645 McKechnie Drive
West Vancouver BC

CONTENTS

ILLUSTRATIONS

ILLUSTRATIONS

8

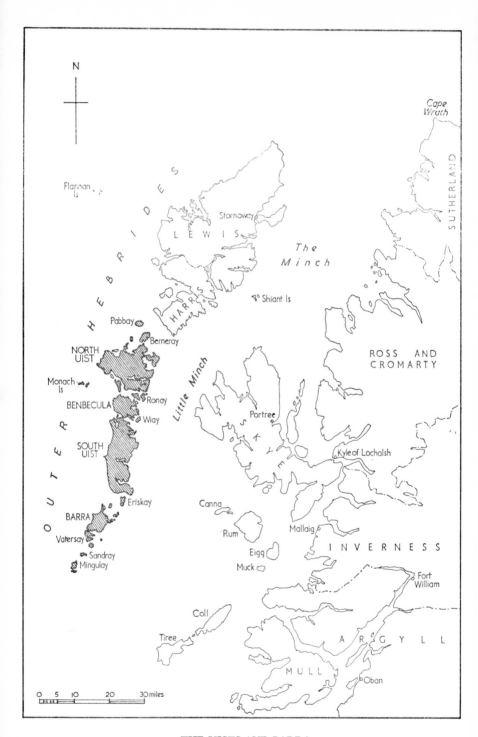

N

Cape
Wrath

SUTHERLAND

Flannan
Is

LEWIS

Stornoway

The
Minch

Shiant Is

HARRIS

Pabbay

Berneray

NORTH
UIST

ROSS AND
CROMARTY

Monach
Is

Little Minch

BENBECULA

Ronay

Wiay

SKYE

Portree

SOUTH
UIST

Kyle of Lochalsh

Eriskay

Canna

BARRA

Rum

Mallaig

Vatersay

Eigg

INVERNESS

Sandray

Muck

Mingulay

Fort
William

Coll

Tiree

A R G Y L L

MULL

Oban

0 5 10   20   30 miles

THE UISTS AND BARRA

1 INTRODUCTION TO THE ISLANDS

THE islands which are the subject of this book form the southern part of the chain of islands off the western seaboard of Scotland known as the Western Isles, the Outer Hebrides, or the Long Island. The main islands are North Uist, Benbecula, South Uist, Eriskay, Barra and Vatersay. Attendant on these are smaller islands, most of which were inhabited once but are now either completely deserted (save for the grazing of sheep) or tenanted by a shepherd during the summer months only. North Uist is now joined to Benbecula by a causeway, and Benbecula to South Uist by a bridge.

The Outer Hebrides generally are composed of ancient gneiss and intrusions of granites and basalts. In many places the gneiss has weathered to a thin and acid soil that supports a blanket of thick peat. Along the western shores of each island lies a belt of sandbars and dunes, whose positioning has been a significant factor in the retention of population for many centuries. Indeed, this belt, or machair, has been responsible for the wide divergences in ecology and land use between the northern and southern parts of the Hebridean chain.

Although the islands in the southern chain of the Hebrides display individual characteristics, there are a number of aspects which bring them together as a group. Their social structure and its development, economic bases, the provision of services such as medicine and education, and the development of mainland-island communications, have all followed much the same pattern. Their climate, flora and fauna are very similar.

THE UISTS AND BARRA

The interconnection of North Uist, Benbecula and South Uist by causeway and bridge, and the ease of travel between them compared with the past, when voyages were dictated by weather and tidal conditions and might take days rather than hours, has tended to unify these three communities. The island of Barra, on the other hand, is unable to participate effectively in the new era of wealth and prosperity which exists in its northern neighbours, and so preserves more of its past ways.

In the past, indeed for the past 15 centuries at least, the small islands of the Southern Hebrides have been part of an integrated pattern of living which finally disappeared only in the early years of the present century, the result of various stresses imposed on the indigenous population from outside the Hebridean area. The Hebridean standard of living fell far below that in Britain as a whole. Unfortunately visitors discovered that the islands were romantic, and wrote about them in such a way that their real social and economic problems were ignored. Their poverty was part of their romantic image. Had there been a realistic social writer at the turn of the century with an eye for the facts, the picture might well have been different today, and island-living, even on the smaller Hebridean islands, might have been accepted by British society in general as commonplace.

Instead, the Hebrideans were projected by well meaning writers to the outside world as 'charming' because of their 'quaint' ways, because their housing standards were out-dated, because their economic bases were limited, and because they lived 'close to nature'. Many islanders were nauseated by the imposed image.

The small number of voters led to Government neglect. Proposals for changes in land use and ideas for development that were ready for implementation at the turn of the century are still being considered today. The islanders have in fact spent the twentieth century trying to catch up with the material prosperity of the rest of Britain. The spiritual aspects of the good life have always been theirs in abundance.

The rest of this introductory chapter deals with communications and services, and with certain common island industries. The succeeding chapters deal with the islands in particular.

COMMUNICATIONS

Joining the Main Islands

Benbecula ceased to be a separate island in 1943 when the South Bridge was opened. Father O'Regan, who was parish priest to the Catholic community on the island at that time, was one of the main proponents of the bridge, which is still known locally as 'O'Regan's Bridge'. It joins South Uist and Benbecula between Carnan and Creagorry, stretching over what was known as the South Ford—sands and shell-beaches that once had to be crossed either on foot or by horse-drawn carriage. The bridge was not built entirely with the needs of the indigenous population in mind. Rather it was constructed to link the port of Lochboisdale in South Uist and the RAF aerodrome at Balivanich on Benbecula.

The North Ford causeway was opened by Her Majesty the Queen Mother in September 1960, joining Gramisdale in Benbecula with Carinish in North Uist, and thus creating a through route of some 70 miles between Pollachar in South Uist and the Sound of Berneray off North Uist.

Both the old fords were dangerous and could be crossed when the tide was out only with an expert guide. The departing traveller always left with a prayer: 'Faothail mhath dhuibh'— 'A good ford to you'. Guides were often hard put to it to trace new safe tracks across the sands after each winter's storms had brought changes. At low tide a pony and trap made the journey, at high tide a motor boat plied between Carinish in North Uist and Gramisdale in Benbecula. The ford is about

4 miles long and follows a roundabout route to avoid quicksands. It was open for about 1hr on either side of low water and the route was marked by beacons and cairns or 'weed-covered stones which show well against the white sand'. It was practicable on foot in fine weather only.

Sea Routes

From the eighteenth century all communications for the southern islands of the Outer Hebrides, including mails, passed through North Uist. The services were provided by Government vessels such as the sloop *Perseverance*. Later the *Skylark* and the cutter *Dawn* provided tri-weekly services and eventually a daily contact. The early mail contracts to and from the Outer Islands were held initially by the Highland Fisheries Co Ltd, which operated the chartered steamers *Tartar* and *Holly*. In 1888 MacBrayne's secured the mail contracts for the Outer Islands.

In the sailing schedules of the various shipping companies which once operated in the Minch waters, the name of Lochmaddy is redolent of a former bygone age. Being the administrative centre for North Uist and offering good harbour facilities, the port almost monopolised the passenger and mail traffic for the island. There have been frequent and regular connections with neighbouring islands and the Scottish mainland, and with Skye in particular.

From about 1750 the mails and passengers were carried by smacks sailing between Dunvegan in Skye and the south-east corner of North Uist, the regular port of call being Bagh Seolaid Rudh' Eubhadh, at the south side of Eaval. Disaster overtook one of these smacks when it foundered just north of Ronay Island with the loss of all on board—and the irreplaceable Presbytery Records of Uist up to the year 1786. In 1840 all mails for South Uist, Eriskay, Barra and Benbecula were routed through Lochmaddy; it seems likely that Harris also was served under subsidies from various proprietors, though by

1846 Harris had its own packet sailing twice weekly in summer and once a week in winter between Tarbert and Uig (Skye). Very early in the nineteenth century a mail packet station was established at Lochmaddy to act as a terminal for the sloop *Perseverance*, which sailed fortnightly from Lochmaddy to Dunvegan in Skye. The story is told of a policeman who had to wait with a prisoner at Lochmaddy for the sloop to appear to take the latter to Inverness to serve a 6 weeks' sentence. This period exhausted itself just as the *Perseverance* made her delayed appearance in the bay, so that a voyage across the Minch became unnecessary.

The service provided by the *Perseverance* was gradually improved by successive weekly, twice-weekly (1827) and thrice-weekly (1837) services of another ship, the *Skylark*. The cutter *Dream*, with great regularity, made a daily round trip between the same ports from 1876 until 1886, when she was superseded by MacBrayne's steamers. The *Dream*, however, made noteworthy history with her 5½ round trips per week throughout her run of 10 years.

Communications with the ports on the Clyde were provided by the *Dunara Castle* and *Hebridean*, which called at Lochmaddy weekly from their base at Glasgow; they also put in at numerous intermediate ports of call. About 1880 a public company was formed to develop the Hebridean fisheries and to put a steamer on the Uists route. The ship left Oban on alternate days thrice weekly, calling also at Coll and Tiree, and thereafter crossing to Castlebay. From there she sailed northwards, calling at Lochboisdale and Lochmaddy, before returning to Oban by the same route. The steamer carried mails, though the great bulk of letters and packets for Uist went via Skye. The Parliamentary Walpole Commission (1888), set up to conduct enquiries into communications in the Western Isles, was followed by an improved steamer service. Under the new arrangements one of David MacBrayne's mail steamers left Oban every Monday, Wednesday and Friday, calling at

Tobermoray (Mull), Castlebay, Lochboisdale and Lochmaddy on the outward passage. Thereafter she crossed the Minch to Skye, and called at Dunvegan, Glendale and Bracadale on her homeward passage, reaching Oban on the following day. On Tuesdays, Thursdays and Saturdays another of MacBrayne's steamers followed the same route.

The present sea link is principally the Hebridean Ferry operated by David MacBrayne, on which the MV *Hebrides* (launched at Aberdeen in 1964 as a sister ship to the *Clansman* and *Columba*) began operation on 15 April 1964. Initially there was only one crossing of the Minch between Uig (Skye) and Lochmaddy per day in each direction; but the ship was soon placed on a full timetable involving two double runs daily. The *Hebrides* replaced the *Lochmor,* which had sailed across the Minch waters for almost 35 years. The Hebridean Ferry berths at Tarbert (Harris) and Lochmaddy on alternate nights, and spends the weekends at Tarbert. The route connects Uig, Tarbert and Lochmaddy.

The passenger movements and freight tonnage at Lochmaddy pier have increased considerably since the ferry was introduced. In 1963 the passengers carried numbered about 2,700, but in 1964, with the ferry service operating, the figure jumped to about 15,000. The number of cars rose from 240 to 3,000. The freight tonnage landed has also increased, but not so spectacularly, reflecting the use made of the ferry by commercial vehicles (zero in 1963 to 130 in 1964 and almost 300 in the following year).

A new ferry, offering for the first time a daily scheduled passenger service through the Sound of Harris, links Newton and Leverburgh, Harris.

Locheport merits a mention as a North Uist port of call, particularly in the years before World War II. Among the varied goods landed were lime, slate, building materials, bedsteads, concrete and iron ranges. The 'exports' included barley, potatoes and kelp.

Page 17 (*above*) Lochboisdale, South Uist, from Ben Kenneth; (*below*) the island steamer *Claymore* lies alongside the pier at Castlebay, with the restored Kiessimul Castle in the background

Page 18 (*above*) Main Street, Castlebay, Barra, with Kiessimul Castle; (*below*) the Haun, Eriskay. South Uist and the Eriskay Sound in the background

One of the Minch maritime lights operated by the Commissioners of Northern Lighthouses is Weaver's Point, at the entrance to Loch Maddy. Erected in 1891, it is now a minor light maintained by the Lighthouse Commissioners on behalf of the Department of Agriculture and Fisheries for Scotland.

South Uist has had a long-established sea connection with the Scottish mainland and neighbouring islands, and the island's ports are not without interest. To the north there is Loch Carnan, an excellent harbour once given up in favour of the dangerous pier constructed at Peter's Port in Benbecula in 1896. The Loch Carnan piers are newly developed, particularly for the use of the army's tank-landing craft. There is a safe anchorage for large steamers, which used to enter the Loch and discharge their cargo into small craft from South Uist and Benbecula.

A couple of miles farther south lies Loch Skiport, whose pier was erected in 1879 by Lady Gordon Cathcart at a cost of £1,950. There is a good clean entrance to the Loch, which has all the appearance of a canal. Before World War II the main activity at the pier was the shipping of sheep for mainland sales. Loch Skiport is the best and the easiest of access of any harbour between Lochmaddy and Lochboisdale. Just south, at Rubha Ushinish, is the lighthouse, established in 1857.

Lochboisdale is the main port in South Uist. Its pier (reconstructed in 1963–4) is the only pier in Scotland owned directly by a District Council. The port has seen much of Hebridean history, such as the embarking, on board the *Admiral*, of 'voluntary' candidates for emigration to Canada in 1851. Loch Boisdale, like most of the island's sea lochs, scatters itself about widely in a great number of creeks, bays and inlets, and has numerous islets and rock-reefs. The tiny island of Gasay tends to shelter the pier entrance. At the southern entrance to the Loch lies the island of Calvay, which supports a minor automatic light, now operated by acetylene. The first light was established there in 1857.

The main traditional route to Lochboisdale is via Mull, Coll, Tiree and Barra. At the present time Lochboisdale is the port for one of the new car-ferry crossings of the Minch. The MacBrayne motor vessel *Claymore* calls on Mondays, Wednesdays and Fridays from Oban. In the summer months the *Clansman*, one of MacBrayne's car ferries (launched at Aberdeen on 16 January 1964, a sister ship to the *Hebrides*) used to make five round trips weekly from Mallaig to Lochboisdale, via Armadale in Skye. This ship entered service in June 1964, but was withdrawn in 1974.

A small ferry operates between Haun on Eriskay and Ludac on South Uist, and it also connects with Eoligary on Barra.

Among the ships of the past which have sailed the Minch waters with calls at Lochboisdale have been the *Dunara Castle*, the *Plover*, the *Cygnet*, the *Hebrides*, and the SY *Killarney*. This last vessel was a cruise ship of 1,200 tons which sailed on different itineraries during the summer months. Her grey hull and yellow funnels were once a common sight in Hebridean ports. When she pulled away from the quayside at Stornoway, the writer remembers, her passengers used to throw coins for the children to scramble after.

The *Clansman* was launched in 1955 from Denny's of Dumbarton, and since then has been almost wholly employed on MacBrayne's Inner Isles Mail Route. A connection was once made at Lochboisdale with the Outer Isles Mail steamer *Lochmor*. Now buses connect Lochboisdale with Lochmaddy to meet mails from the *Hebrides*.

Among the early ships to become familiar sights to the folk of Barra was the TSS *Flowerdale*, MacBrayne's first twin-screw sea-going steamer. She, along with the *Staffa*, was stationed at Oban. Each ship left on alternate weekday mornings to give a daily service. The *Flowerdale* was lost off Lismore in 1904, her machinery and boilers being salved for installation in the SS *Cygnet*. This latter ship formed one half of a tandem service for the Outer Isles with her sister ship SS *Plover*, the recipient of the second boiler and port engines salved from the *Flowerdale*.

These two ships conducted the Islands mail services from 1918 until the advent of the new motor vessels in 1930. One ship operated from Oban (outwards on Mondays, Wednesdays and Fridays) to Coll, Tiree, Castlebay and Lochboisdale; while the other, from Kyle of Lochalsh, worked both north and south of Skye via Mallaig, embracing Eigg, Rum, Canna, Lochboisdale, Lochmaddy and Harris.

From 1930 the Islands mail service was provided by the sister ships TSMV *Lochearn* and TSMV *Lochmor*, two additions to MacBrayne's when the company became David MacBrayne (1928) Limited. It had an obligation to build not fewer than four ships within 2 years, and its contract also demanded improvements in the Outer Islands services as regards passenger accommodation, coupled with lower fares and freight charges. In 1964 both ships were sold to Greek owners.

At the end of the nineteenth century three companies operated services among the Hebridean islands—David MacBrayne, Martin Orme & Co, and John MacCallum. The latter two interests merged, and were eventually absorbed in 1947 into MacBrayne's, who now have almost a monopoly of inter-island and mainland-island routes.

The *St Clair of the Isles* was one of the MacCallum ships, running weekly, from 1873, from Glasgow to the Outer Hebrides and the more distant parts of Skye. The route varied each week: on one trip calls were made at Dunvegan and Uig first, then Lochmaddy and Lochboisdale; and on another trip this order was reversed, and calls were also made at Port Charlotte, Bowmore, Small Isles (Jura), Coll, Islay, Barra and Port Phaedair. The SS *Dunara Castle* belonged to the combined MacCallum–Orme fleet. She was a well known sight in Hebridean waters, pushing her 500 tons through heavy Minch swells, entering silent little lochs to discharge a cargo, or anchoring off some small township to take on sheep or cattle. With her sister ship the SS *Hebrides* (which belonged to MacCallum before the merger with Martin Orme), these two vessels brought the outside world to the doorstep of many otherwise isolated communities. The *Dunara Castle* made her last voyage to the west Highlands in 1948, just after the combined MacCallum–Orme fleet passed to MacBrayne, and was broken up during the summer of that year.

The present mainland/island link, between Oban and Castlebay, is provided by the TSMV *Claymore*. Launched in 1955 she is provided with modern aids to navigation and has accommodation for almost 500 passengers, with sleeping accommodation for fifty-six. The *Claymore*'s route is Oban, Tobermoray, Coll, Tiree, Castlebay, Lochboisdale and return.

The lifeboat station at Castlebay forms part of the network of sea-rescue services for the Minch waters. The lifeboat has provided other services in its time, such as taking emergency medical cases to the Bute Hospital on South Uist.

Barra Head lighthouse, established in 1833, is situated on the west side of Berneray. Buoys and beacons (five in all) are placed in strategic positions to complement land-based lights operated either by electricity or propane gas. The whole of the sea area around Barra, particularly on its eastern side, is littered with small islands, islets, rocks, reefs and undersea shoals which are barely exposed even at low water. They have taken their due toll of ships, perhaps the most famous being the *Politician* (see p 164).

Air Links

Balivanich (Baile-mhanaich—the Monks' Town, where there was once a monastery with a grant of lands from one of the Lords of the Isles) in Benbecula is the air terminus for the Southern Hebrides, developed from the World War II aerodrome established by the RAF. Air travel in the Hebrides has been taken for granted by the islanders for over 30 years now and has proved to be of significant value in making these islands less remote. It takes less time to get to London by air from Balivanich (2½hr) than it does by road from many towns and cities in southern England. The air route south is also used for freight, particularly lobsters, for which there is a good market in London and on the Continent. Flights direct to the Continent are normal.

There has, however, been a gradual decline in the number of passengers at Balivanich, possibly reflecting the effect of alternative routes, via vehicle ferries, to the Hebrides. The present figure of about 14,000 passengers per annum is a decrease of some 2,500 from the 1963 figure.

The history of the Western Highlands air services is told in Capt E. Fresson's *Air Road to the Isles*. The original flights were from Glasgow to Islay and Campbeltown. These were extended in 1935 to South Uist, the plane landing at Askernish, thus establishing the first scheduled air service to the Outer Islands. The building of the RAF airfield at Balivanich brought Benbecula into the picture, and it was used by BEA en route to Stornoway. Since 1947 the planes operating over the Outer Isles routes have changed from Rapides to Dakotas. The present British airways service uses Viscounts, with six return flights throughout the year (Glasgow/Benbecula/Stornoway and return). A service is also provided between Glasgow and Stornoway, with a landing at Balivanich, by Loganair Ltd, for freight and charter passengers. This Glasgow-based company has proved that an inter-island air service can pay its way, bringing in such commodities as newspapers, electrical goods, drapery, motor car spares, flowers and foodstuffs, and flying out tweed, knitwear and shellfish. The company also undertakes useful charter work. With the recent increase in the number of landing fields throughout the Hebrides, Loganair is able to provide a linking service for British airways in the form of air-taxi services that can be booked with the British airways ticket.

On the great 'Cockle Ebb' on Traigh Mhor is Barra Airfield, probably one of the most beautiful and most unusual in Britain. Once each day from April to September, and three times weekly (weather permitting) during the remainder of the year, a small aircraft lands and leaves. The timetable is regulated by the tides. The plane, a DH Heron, takes about 1hr to reach Barra from Glasgow Airport, the combined service linking Glasgow, Tiree, Barra, then returning.

Barra's first experience of a commercial air service began in 1935. In the previous year Northern & Scottish Airways Ltd was formed, with a capital of £7,000, and the company's first air route took in Campbeltown and Islay. The next year saw the start of a circular return service between Glasgow, Skye, North Uist, South Uist, Barra and Glasgow. In 1937 Scottish Airways Ltd was formed by the amalgamation of the above company and Highland Airways Ltd, a service mainly used by the Orkneys and Shetland. In 1946 the Civil Aviation Act came into effect to regulate British internal airlines, and in 1947 a Scottish Division of BEA was given the islands routes.

The air-ambulance service which operates between the Western Isles and the Scottish mainland, flying de Haviland aircraft, was set up in 1935 by the County Councils responsible for the islands' administration. The service has been a tremendous success, and many islanders are alive today because of its speed and efficiency.

Delays to flights caused by tides on Traigh Mhor, Barra, have led to agitation for a permanent airfield; and one of the first moves was a survey carried out by the army, through their OPMAC scheme (Operation Programme, Military Aid to the Community). This survey revealed that an airstrip at Eoligarry was a feasible project, at an estimated cost of £80,000, of which sum the Highlands and Islands Development Board would pay half. But a further survey in 1971 considered that substantial wind and sea erosion threatened to cut a channel through the proposed site and turn Eoligarry peninsula into an island. The Barra Council of Social Service disputed the findings, stating that the families in the area had many years' experience of the movements of the sand dunes and were unable to see how the experts had arrived at their conclusion. The matter of the new airstrip awaits a final assessment of the evidence, while other sites are being considered at Borve.

While as yet possessing no airport, North Uist has nevertheless been in air communication with the other Hebridean islands and with the Scottish mainland for over 30 years. The island's landing strip was at Sollas, one of the hopping and stopping-off places used by small chartered aircraft from Glasgow (Renfrew Airport). The first air services were operated by Northern & Scottish Airways Ltd, which intended to provide a permanent schedule of flights to and from the islands. It was planned to have a plane based on Sollas Airport (as it was called) as an inter-island facility, and to give the airport its own wireless station. An air-ambulance service operated by the company rendered extremely valuable aid to patients and doctors. The company was amalgamated with Highland Airways, as we have seen.

The present landing strip at Sollas is used by Loganair Ltd for charter flights. Though there has been local agitation for a helicopter ambulance service, the Board of Trade has rejected pleas for this on the grounds that helicopters cannot achieve the same high standard of safety as fixed-wing aircraft.

POPULATION

The population figures for the last two centuries or so for the Southern Hebrides show the familiar steady increase for such islands from the mid-eighteenth century to the mid-nineteenth, and thereafter a decline, beginning with a drop during the period of the clearances, which were commonplace throughout the Hebrides in the last century. The maximum population, and the beginnings of rise and fall, vary for each island, showing that local factors operated, though the pattern was recognisable throughout the group.

THE UISTS AND BARRA

The islands of the Southern Hebrides are administered by the Western Isles Regional Authority. Politically, the islands form part of the Western Isles Constituency, formed in 1918. The present Member of Parliament, an adherent of the Scottish National Party, won the seat in 1970 from the previous Labour Member, who had held it for 35 years without change, and retained it in 1974. The Court House at Lochmaddy, North Uist, deals with cases which come within the jurisdiction of the Sheriff.

As in other parts of Britain, the County Council supplies a travelling book service—a book van, manned by a librarian and an assistant, which travels between North and South Uist, with collections for Barra being sent across Barra Sound. Where the service is different, however, is in its selection of books, for probably no other carries such a proportion of Gaelic publications—fiction, poetry and non-fiction.

ELECTRICITY, WATER AND FIRE SERVICES

A public electricity supply (4,500kW), provided by the North of Scotland Hydro-electric Board, was generated at the diesel power station at Daliburgh, South Uist. This station has now been phased out of use with the construction of a new station (7,600kW) at Loch Carnan, South Uist. The new station will meet a demand for electricity that is increasing at about 9 per cent per annum. Most of the load is domestic, the industrial and non-domestic load being derived from the seaweed processing factories at Orasay and Sponish (North Uist), the lobster storage pond at Grimsay, and the Balivanich airport on Benbecula. Just under 80 per cent of the houses on South Uist are connected to mains electricity. A similar percentage applies to North Uist, which includes Baleshare and Grimsay islands; the supply was switched on only in 1969 after some

26

20 years of waiting. The Barra load is supplied through a submarine cable across the Sound of Barra and about 70 per cent of the houses have mains electricity.

The public water supply on the islands forms part of the scheme developed throughout the Hebrides to supply rural piped water to virtually all island townships. In North Uist the supply is taken from the Ben Lee reservoir. The South Uist supply is mostly taken from Loch Fhiarain, which lies to the south-west of Beinn Mhor. The Barra water supply is obtained from a reservoir created by a dam across Loch an Duin, in the northern part of the island, and from Loch Uisge, just above Castlebay.

A Fire Brigade station is located at Lochmaddy, and has a complement of ten men volunteers under the charge of a station officer.

MEDICAL SERVICES

The ancient medical services available to the people of the Highlands and Islands were provided by itinerant and hereditary physicians who belonged to families attached to the chiefs of clans and whose learning and skill was passed from father to son over many generations. The MacBeths and Beatons (first mentioned in the eleventh century) were well known in the Gaelic west of Scotland and in the Islands as physicians. The oldest Gaelic manuscript on medical matters bears the date AD 1403. Though largely confined to the prominent clan families, the services of these physicians were also available to the poorer members of a clan, though the mass of the population relied mostly on folk cures, many of which are being increasingly acknowledged as effective.

The first formal step towards the provision of health services was taken by the Poor Law (Scotland) Amendment Act of 1845, which placed upon parishes the duty of seeing that 'there shall be proper and sufficient Arrangements made for dispensing and supplying Medicines to the sick Poor' and of securing 'proper Medical Attendance for the Inmates of every . . . Poorhouse'. By the same Act parishes were empowered to subscribe to hospitals, and parochial boards were required 'to provide for Medicines, Medical Attendance, nutritious Diet, Cordials and Clothing for such Poor, in such Manner and to such Extent as may seem equitable and expedient'. These statutory provisions were, in fact, of little relevance to the conditions prevailing in the Highlands, and more particularly, in the Islands; it was not sufficiently realised that where cash played little part in the local economy and the rateable values were relatively low, a gross disparity existed between parish obligations and the resources available to meet these.

Better medical provisions came early in the twentieth century, following the creation of the Highlands and Islands Medical Service Committee (the Dewar Committee), which prevailed on Parliament to establish the Highlands and Islands Medical Service Fund 'for improving medical services, including nursing, in the Highlands and Islands of Scotland, and otherwise providing and improving means for the prevention, treatment and alleviation of illness and suffering therein'. Under the Act grants were approved to provide doctors and nurses; specialist, hospital and ambulance services; and telegraph and telephone services.

Many of the illnesses on South Uist were derived from the insanitary conditions in which the people lived, and the crofters and cottars had no incentive to improve their living conditions. One common practice was the housing of cattle under the same roof as the human occupants, and in 1891 70 per cent of the houses fell into this category. In 1892 the Medical Officer for Inverness wrote: 'Dr Macintyre [then the local Medical Officer], South Uist, informs me that a great many children, and even adults, have suffered from internal parasites got from drinking stagnant and polluted water, which too often is their only water supply.' This bad water resulted in fevers, but, strangely, there was a low rate of mortality, less than 10 persons per 1,000 of the population. 'On the face of it, this appears a highly satisfactory state for the public health to be in, but I regret to report that during the whole year there has been existent in the district an epidemic of the disease which, par excellence, is the test of sanitation, viz., enteric fever . . .'

The Bute Hospital, at Daliburgh, was erected in 1894, at the expense of the Marchioness of Bute and she maintained it for a number of years. It was superintended by nuns with hospital training, the local doctor being called in when his services were required, and was open to all denominations. In 1899 there were sixty-six patients who cost 3s per day each. Out-patients were visited by the nuns. Another building was converted into a hospital for infectious diseases as the result of a serious outbreak of typhus, particularly virulent in South Uist and Eriskay.

At present Bute Hospital has fourteen beds, ten of which are general unallocated and four are for maternity cases; the Long Island Hospital at Lochmaddy has forty beds, thirty-five for mentally and five for chronic sick; and the Hospice, also at Lochmaddy, caters for maternity cases. There is no hospital on Barra. Each of the islands has its doctors, supported by the District Nursing Service. In addition, the hospital facilities available at Inverness and Glasgow are used by island patients.

A chiropodist visits North Uist twice each year, a service arranged by the local Branch of the British Red Cross. Social services are also provided by the local authority, and non-official Councils of Social Service have recently been established in the islands. There is an old people's home, Uist House, at Daliburgh.

As one would expect in the primitive conditions which existed in Barra a century ago, certain diseases and ills were always part and parcel of island life. Water, particularly when obtained from a surface well, was an excellent disease-carrier, though Barra tradition makes little mention of waterborne epidemics. Measles, whooping cough and scarlet fever were known specifically, but other ailments were classed as 'fevers'. The latter were often derived from visitors, who brought viruses against which the islanders had little or no resistance. Outbreaks of typhoid or typhus were common, but they never reached epidemic proportions. One primitive form of cleansing affected houses comprised burning sulphur in a saucer to fumigate them. No doubt many cures were of the 'faith' variety.

The first doctor to reside in Barra was Dr McGillivray, who arrived in the mid-nineteenth century, though he was more concerned with his estate at Eoligarry than the health of the islanders. Before his arrival Barra was visited periodically by doctors, and surgeons came from time to time by revenue cutter. One common complaint needing surgery was epitheliomata, in which a growth on the lip had to be excised. This complaint, it was thought, derived from the Barra men's fondness for heavy smoking of clay pipes, and was probably caused by the tar products in the tobacco.

Tubercular infection was known, though its nature was not, and many people suffered needlessly from consumption, and infection of the bones, joints and lymphatic glands, often referred to as the King's Evil.

HOUSING

The traditional form of thatched dwelling is still extensively used in South Uist, perhaps more so than in the rest of the Outer Hebrides. Modern standards of living apply, however, and only in their outward appearance are these present-day structures the traditional houses described in the literature of the past two centuries.

The *New Statistical Account for Scotland* (1837) notes that there were fifteen houses with slated roofs in South Uist, and continues:

The people are remarkably clean in their habits. Though far from woods their houses in general are more capacious and in every respect of a better description than the habitations of many of the same class in more favoured situations. Many of these have their chimneys and their glass windows, and their beds boxed with timber at the back, on the top, and at both ends; and all sweep and sand their earthen floors daily.

By 1881 there were still further improvements in housing standards, though many buildings were regarded as being inferior. In 1887

... they were oblong structures, rounded at the corners and built with undressed stone, generally without mortar. The gables were of the same height as the side elevations. Above the gable wall the cabers sloped inwards at the same angle as the cabers rising from the side walls, so that the roof of a house whose length was not much greater than its breadth presented the appearance of a dome. There was usually a small window, and sometimes two, to admit light. Formerly houses without windows were quite common. There were 50 of these in South Uist in 1871, but by 1881 they had been reduced to 5 [they had disappeared altogether by 1891]. The interior usually consisted of two apartments. The main apartment, with a fire in the middle of the floor and a lum, or chimney, right above it to carry away the smoke, was occupied by the inmates during the day. Over the fire, a chain, with pot-hook, was suspended from a cross-beam, and on a wet day the rain coming in fell about the fire. The floor was of mud. The atmosphere inside was charged with soot. The other apartment was used as a bedroom. Not infrequently there was a third area in which the cattle were housed. The walls were about seven feet high, and the partitions inside were not carried up to the roof.

Subsequent developments included roofs of tarred felt, zinc, corrugated iron, or slate. The former rounded corners became more angular, and the fire was placed at a gable end with properly constructed chimney breasts. Two-storey houses became common, with two rooms and a closet downstairs, and two attics, sometimes converted into sleeping accommodation, upstairs.

The practice of housing cattle under the same roof as the family was common in 30 per cent of the houses in Benbecula in 1891. These conditions produced a continual stream of illnesses, but by 1905 the practice had been virtually abolished.

Accounts of Barra written towards the end of the eighteenth century and in the early nineteenth frequently describe the people as living in abject poverty, in houses which were primitive and unhygienic. Barra, in fact, was overcrowded. At the turn of the present century it was one of the worst of the congested districts in the Highlands, and even as late as 1931 the average density of population for the island was 64·3 per square mile, compared with about 35 for the Outer Hebrides generally. Up until about 1870 there were no mortar-built houses on the island, excepting a manse, the priest's house, Eoligarry House and one old building in Castlebay which served first as a merchant's store and later as a licensed premises.

Local authority accommodation now exists on all the islands, for those who have no crofts, 'key' workers, and for young families who have severed their ties with the parents' crofts. Houses are also provided by the North of Scotland Hydro-electric Board for its employees. The army on North and South Uist and Benbecula has erected large housing estates for its personnel. There are also a number of private houses on the islands.

EDUCATION

In May 1866 came the publication of a description of life in the Western Isles by Alexander Nicolson, himself a Gaelic-speaking Highlander, who had been assigned the task of reporting to a Royal Commission on the State of Education in the Hebrides. To Lowlanders this Gaelic-speaking area was so remote that, in the words of one of Her Majesty's Inspectors of Schools, a transfer to it was regarded 'with disappointment, as a kind of banishment to a boreal darkness'. Nicolson visited twenty-three Hebridean islands under conditions reminiscent of Dr Samuel Johnson's tour some 80 years previously. At a time when literacy (particularly in English) was taken for granted in most of the country districts of Scotland, in the Hebrides, according to marriage registers, only half the men and one-third of the women could write their names. Because they could not speak English, they were unable to release themselves from a life of poverty by seeking work elsewhere. If they crossed to the Scottish mainland, they were in the 'predicament of dumb persons; and their sensitiveness to ridicule often exposes them to the pain of being reckoned barbarians . . .' Nicolson urged that children in the Hebrides should be first taught in their home tongue and then in English. He found that the English language was taught so unimaginatively that few in the schools could read it with understanding. Many teachers considered the use of Gaelic 'a mark of rusticity', so that the children were invariably spoken to in what was to them a foreign language.

On the other hand, many island parents were apathetic about education, and those who did send their children to the local school kept them away for the usual seasonal occupations— herding cattle, gathering seaweed, cutting and drying peat, and collecting bait for fisherfolk. Nicolson, who was moved by the waste of talent, wrote: 'The pleasure I experienced in witnessing so much of bright and eager intelligence was often mixed with pain at seeing it associated with poverty and raggedness and thinking how many of these intelligent children, fit for better things, would in the course of a few years, simply for the want of a fair start, be inevitably metamorphosed into day labourers and fishermen.'

South Uist

Before the passing of the Education Act in 1872 schools in South Uist were provided and maintained by various philan-

33

thropic bodies such as the Church of Scotland and the Ladies' Association of the United Free Church of Scotland. In 1811 the Gaelic Schools Society founded a school at Frobost, South Uist, and 15 years later there were three schools on the island. By 1837 the figure had risen to ten schools, which number included one parochial, seven maintained by various bodies, and two schools to which girls were sent to be taught sewing and to learn to read Gaelic. In 1843 there were no less than eight schools supported by the Ladies' Association, and it is on record that no religious difficulty arose between the Protestant teachers and the Catholic children. In fact, a number of South Uist boys of the Catholic faith subsequently entered the priesthood after receiving their education in the Free Church Schools. The reason was that the schools were established to provide education without any ulterior motives of conversion.

The number of schools on South Uist tended to fluctuate as their founders encountered more or less difficulty in finding cash and teachers to keep them going. The average school population was twenty-five. Regular attendance was the exception rather than the rule; apart from the various domestic duties the children were expected to carry out, bad weather, illness and the like kept the children away from all but a rudimentary education.

Then religious intolerance, which, as we have seen, had been kept at bay, took charge, in South Uist in particular; for the responsibility for education and its administration, even after 1872, fell into the hands of partisan Protestants.

Reverting to the eighteenth century, many schools throughout the Highlands, much of which was Catholic in some degree, were established by the Society in Scotland for the Propagation of Christian Knowledge (SSPCK), which was formed in 1709 for the purpose of establishing such schools to extirpate the Gaelic language and the Catholic religion). Schools with a Catholic background did exist, however, as the minutes of meetings of the SSPCK on 16 March 1727 reveal:

Page 35   (*above*) Crofts near Ersary, Barra; (*below*) the Cockle Strand (Traigh Mhor), Barra

Page 36 (above) Mingulay village and road to the landing bay (top left). The school-house (top centre) is used by crofters from Barra when sheep shearing; (below) Village Bay, Eriskay

The Committee Reported that they had a Letter from the presbytery of Long Island [the Outer Hebrides] with two representations, one concerning the State of Southuist and Bara united into one parish, and giving an account of the bounds thereof, and of the Catechisable persons in every district, and shewing that they are all papists except a very few, and pitching upon the places where Schools may be settled, and shewing that there are two popish schools therein.

[The Committee] recommended to Mr Alex. MacLeod and Mr Alexander Mitchell to speak to Mr Alex. MacKenzie of Delvine purchaser of the estate of Clan Ronald and Doctor Dundas & Monzie to speak to the Sollicitor to use the proper measures to for suppressing the forsaid popish Schools.

The MacKenzie of Delvine mentioned above was the nominal purchaser on behalf of the Clanranald family. The Committee renewed its recommendation for the suppression of the Catholic schools in South Uist on 8 and 26 June 1727.

When one questions why it was not possible for parents to exercise some control over their children's education, it must be remembered that lack of freedom and security prevented them taking any action. Even after 1872, this right, which was made available to them in law, could not be exercised without serious consideration of the possible repercussions, such as instant eviction, without any compensation, by the estate authorities. Again, under the penal laws there had been little possibility of Catholic education developing in Scotland. The matter was righted only after the passing of the Crofters' Act in 1886, which conferred on crofters security of tenure and the right to exercise their franchise.

The new freedom was seen in the early spring of 1888 when an election took place for the election of the School Board in South Uist. Four Catholics and three Protestants were elected. A record of the event says that though the day had been bitterly cold, only three of the 'south end' (Daliburgh parish) people stayed away from the poll, and these were hopelessly feeble. 'The manner and bearing of the people was most consoling to one who has been even only a few years here. They spoke out manfully and defiantly—a great contrast to the last election.' Consequently, the first Catholic headmaster was appointed— F. G. Rea to Garrynamonie school. The difficulty then was in finding Catholic teachers qualified in secondary education subjects.

At the present time South Uist has seven schools, including two junior secondary schools (at Iochdar and Daliburgh). Four schools have been closed by the County Authority since 1959.

Benbecula

There were four schools in Benbecula in the middle of the last century, but only one was really active—that maintained by the Glasgow Free Church Ladies' Association. Later, before the 1872 Education Act, the schools were provided by the Church of Scotland and the Ladies' Association of the United Free Church. The schools had the usual history of poor attendance resulting from bad weather, bad roads, and children's ailments. After 1872 the four schools then extant were taken over by the Schools Board.

Present-day primary education in Benbecula is catered for by schools at Balivanich, Kilerivagh near Hacklett, and Torlum. Junior secondary schools are available either on North or South Uist. Gaelic is taught in all these schools, as in the rest of the Outer Isles, and is used in varying degrees for general tuition in the usual school subjects.

The increase in the school population through the incoming military has placed serious pressures on accommodation, particularly in the school at Balivanich. Children were taught in corridors and, later, in temporary classrooms. A new primary school to cope with the situation is projected, to be built on reclaimed land obtained by compulsory order from an upset Balivanich crofter who has already lost some 10 acres to military housing. The army must live somewhere, but compulsory orders on good crofting land are resented.

North Uist

North Uist has had provisions for formal education for some two centuries. In 1837 there were eleven schools—a parish school and ten others maintained by various religious and philanthropic bodies. The parish schoolmaster earned £34 4s 4½d annually, plus school fees amounting to a further £16. The Disruption in the Church of Scotland in 1843 gave a fresh impetus to education in the island. The Free Church became active in setting up new schools, which by 1864 brought the total number to sixteen. The average attendance was twenty-five pupils per school, though the four schools provided by the Gaelic Schools Society averaged forty. Most of the schools were thatched buildings with only rudimentary educational provisions. The Education Act of 1872 brought the Schools Board into existence, and that body set about bringing existing accommodation up to reasonable standards. In 1903 there were thirteen schools in North Uist, with a school in each of the islands of Boreray, Baleshare and Grimsay. The last two schools were reached by crossing a ford at low water.

There are at present eight schools in North Uist, including Baleshare: seven of these are primary schools, and the eighth is a junior secondary school at Paible. Three schools have been closed down in the last decade, the last being that on Grimsay, which action by the Inverness-shire Education Committee met with a great deal of unavailing opposition. The Grimsay children now go to Kallin School. The present total school population in North Uist is about 300 pupils. The decrease in school population during the last 70 years is seen by comparing the figures of 1903 with those of the present day (in brackets): Tigharry School 90 (14); Dunskellar School 90 (13); Grimsay 70 (9 in 1969 and now closed); Baleshare 50 (7).

Barra

Until the passing of the Education Act in 1872, the education of children was an optional extra to life on Barra, though many parents took advantage of such facilities as were provided from time to time by various bodies. Towards the end of the eighteenth century the SSPCK was conducting a school on the island. Then the Gaelic Schools Society, founded in Edinburgh in the early nineteenth century and supported by charitable contributions, established a foothold in the provision of itinerant teachers who remained in one district long enough to enable pupils to acquire the groundwork necessary for reading, though the reading matter was mainly Biblical. Instruction and reading were both in Gaelic. In 1882 education was made compulsory, continuous and systematic, though in Barra some degree of gentle persuasion, in the form of the presence of the 'Compulsory' Officer, had to be administered. Three schools were erected, at points roughly equidistant round the island's circular road. Children marched barefooted to school, in winter carrying a few peats for the school fire. The schools were administered by a local School Board, and financed principally from a Government grant that fluctuated according to the school attendance and the tenor of the annual report of a visiting Schools Inspector.

The present-day provision includes three primary schools (at Breivig, Craigston and Eoligarry) and a junior secondary school at Castlebay. These have a total of about 300 pupils, catered for by just under twenty teachers. Despite the lack of higher educational facilities, Barra has sent many of its men into the professional world, in particular as Catholic priests.

The closure of small rural schools is a problem in many areas on the Scottish mainland, and is no less serious on Barra. A number of small primary schools have been closed over the years or else have suffered from the decrease in the island's population. Craigston school, for instance, had ninety-six pupils in 1876, but in 1970 the roll was down to twenty-six, and the school at Balnabodach, which no longer exists, had no less than 114 pupils in 1876 (in which year Castlebay had 141).

INTRODUCTION TO THE ISLANDS

The evolution of a distinct pattern of economic activity in the islands of the Southern Hebrides was a slow process, emerging from what was in general a subsistence economy in which the needs of a community had to be satisfied before any surplus could be exported. Some islands, however, have shown from an early period an inclination towards one kind of activity specially suited to the environment. North Uist over the past two centuries or so has had a fairly well balanced economy, upset in the eighteenth century by its becoming the focal point in the islands for the prosecution of the kelp industry. South Uist, on the other hand, while participating to a significant degree in kelping, had an old established tradition of exporting agricultural products, made possible by a higher degree of fertility (due to the belt of machair on the west side of the island) than its neighbours.

One might naturally expect from islands a deep interest in fishing, but the nature of the social system, which was introduced late in its existence to a cash economy, prevented any attempt to develop it in the Southern Hebrides. This was in fact left (1) to the Dutch and (2) to the Scots from the north and east coasts of Scotland. The islands benefited little from it.

Crofting and fishing are dealt with in the chapters on the different islands, and here we shall deal with other industries.

The Old Kelp Industry

For the Highlands and Islands of Scotland, the kelp industry was both a blessing and a curse. While it lasted, it halted a serious numerical decline in the population by providing work, though it was more profitable for landowners than for the common folk. It was a curse in that its demise left the region seriously overpopulated, with consequent widespread distress among the unemployed.

The roots of the kelp industry go back to the early eighteenth century, when the introduction of manufacturing industry into the Scottish lowlands proved to be something of an advantage to the Highlands region. Glass-making, for instance, required alkali as a basic raw material, and in 1700 a scheme was considered for the establishment of a soap-works in Glasgow, which would need wood-ash. Fern-ash for glass and wood-ash for soap could be obtained in the Western Highlands. But as early as 1569 there are references to the use of kelp (aschen) in the smelting operations of the Geran copper mines near Keswick. In 1688 it was noted that the shores of the Orkney Islands produced 'plenty of tangle of which in other places is made kelp for the making of soap'. The first kelp produced in Scotland, in fact, was made in Orkney, where it was introduced by James Fea, of Whitehall in Stronsay, an Orkney island.

The industry was introduced to the Outer Hebrides about 1735, though Martin Martin in 1695 had made some suggestions regarding the use to which seaweed could be put. That relating to kelp, however, was the only one adopted.

The credit of introducing kelp-making to the Outer Hebrides is given to Hugh MacDonald, of Baleshare Island off the west coast of North Uist. He contracted with an Irishman (the Irish were familiar with the industry) called Roderick MacDonald to get the industry started, and reaped such huge profits that his example was not long ignored by other Highland and Island proprietors. By 1785 many thousands of tons were being produced each year. Two years later the industry received a boost when the duty on barilla was raised to 105s per ton, with a corresponding increase in the price per ton asked for kelp. (Barilla, like kelp, produces alkali on burning.) The wars in Europe also helped the industry, in that they interrupted the import of barilla and placed a scarcity value on kelp.

The main sources of kelp in the Hebrides were North and South Uist and Barra, Harris and Lewis contributing only to a lesser extent. The average output per annum from the Uists for the period 1764 to 1822 was about 800 tons. Barra contributed some 60 tons. North Uist was the focal point for the industry, in 1812 the net proceeds from the island exceeding £14,000. Thousands of workers were employed during the months of June, July and August.

The price of kelp had remained high until 1812, when it began to fall back. Thereafter, under the influence of the revived Spanish trade after the Peninsular War, prices began to plummet. In 1817 the reduction of the duty on salt struck a serious blow at the industry, since salt could perform the same function as kelp; and a further blow resulted in 1822 when Vansittart reduced the import duty on barilla from 220s per cwt to 160s. The whole of the Highlands protested but to no avail, and indeed, in the following year, the duty was further reduced to 100s per cwt. The kelp industry fell into decline, and when the duty was totally repealed by Peel in 1845, there was virtually no kelp industry in the Western Highlands to feel the effect.

The average cost of making one ton of kelp (which needed 24 tons of seaweed) was 45s, freight and other charges amounted to 25s, while the selling price reached a high peak of £22 per ton. At the height of the kelp boom some 50,000 people were employed keeping up to forty vessels laden with Highland kelp busy in the port of London. Kelp workers received 1s per day.

The first documentary reference to kelp is in 1794, a mention by the Rev MacQueen in his contribution to the *Old Statistical Account of Scotland*. Speaking of Barra, he says:

> . . . Formerly the seaweed that grows upon the shore was used for manure; but since kelp has become so valuable, the proprietors everywhere have restricted the people of cutting it for that purpose, which is certainly prejudicial to agriculture . . . The tenants pay their rents by manufacturing kelp and sale of their cattle. The proprietor employs a number of them in making kelp upon his farm, for which he pays from £1, 10s to £2, 2s., and for the kelp made upon their own shores, which he has at

his disposal, £2, 12s 6d. the ton, which is the highest manufacturing price given in the Highlands, so far as I know. So that, from the sale of their cattle, and making of kelp, the people live very easy . . .

In a later statement MacQueen mentions that some 2,000 tons of kelp were sent each year to markets at Liverpool and Leith, and that these fetched the best price that was given for any kelp sent from any part of the Highlands. About 40 years later, in his contribution to the *New Statistical Account for Scotland*, the Rev Nicholson mentions that in 1840 the only manufacture carried out in Barra was that of kelp, 'in which all hands, young and old, are employed for about eight or nine weeks, at £1, 15s or £2 per ton, but for which they formerly received £4, 4s. per ton. Kelp, which on former occasions sold at from £16 to £20 per ton, is now reduced to £2, 10s. or £4 per ton at market, from barilla and salt being used as substitutes for it.'

Alginates

During the period between World Wars I and II the Outer Hebrides experienced a general socio-economic decline, in which, among other economic interests, the collection of seaweed waned considerably. In 1943, however, the interest in seaweed as a natural resource of economic importance was revived. An organisation with the backing of Cefoil Ltd, later to become Alginate Industries Ltd, was set up to collect seaweed from the shores of South Uist and Benbecula to be taken to drying and milling plants on the west coast of the Kintyre (Mull) peninsula. The seaweed was to be turned into an alginate transparent foil and, later, alginate yarn.

The company found difficulty in persuading crofters that it was worth their while to collect the weed, but was eventually able to erect a processing plant at Orasay, near North Boisdale, South Uist. In 1945, supplies were insufficient to keep the plant in operation and 1,000 tons of air-dried weed were imported from Connemara in Eire. This act aroused no little indignation.

But the point was made and taken, and the plant thereafter received sufficient local weed.

Another body, the Institute of Seaweed Research, based in Inverness, was active in experimenting with chemical derivatives as well as surveying seaweed beds during the period 1944–56. After this latter date the research was carried out by the alginate industry itself or at universities. The laboratories of the Institute were acquired in 1957 by a non-profitmaking research group financed by British and American interests, now known as the Arthur D. Little Research Institute, based at Musselburgh.

The present Scottish alginate industry is the second largest of its kind in the world, after the United States. Its total of 1,200 employees includes those workers in the Outer Hebrides who either man the plants or collect the seaweed, though the latter are more correctly self-employed.

The industry in North Uist is focused in the Sponish factory of Alginate Industries (Scotland) Limited, which was opened in 1957 for the production of Ascophyllum meal. It employs twelve men full-time, supported by about twenty-five collectors of raw weed, commonly known as rockweed. 'Tangle' or laminaria is also collected, mostly on South Uist.

The tangle is gathered after it has been washed ashore by winter gales. It is then air-dried on the beaches and bought in this condition for further drying and milling. Rockweed is a year-round crop, cut from rocks at low tide and towed in large rafts by small boats to various bays and inlets, whence it is taken to the factory at Sponish or the sister factory at Orasay, South Uist.

The Highlands and Islands Development Board have given grants for the building of seaweed-collection boats and most of the balance is provided by Alginate Industries in the form of a 4 year loan, repayable from collectors' earnings. Ten of these boats are at present in operation in the Uists and Barra. Rockweed is also collected from the west coast of Scotland, from

Sutherland to Loch Moidart, and in Skye, and taken by the company's boats to its factory at Keose in Lewis or to Sponish. This supply has enabled the Sponish factory to operate on a three-shift basis for the past 3 years, and any surplus seaweed has been diverted to the South Uist base to enable it also to operate over much longer periods.

This factory, like the North Uist factory at Sponish, is supplied with raw weed collected by crofters, and offers full-time employment to twelve men. Recently seaweed collecting has been taken up by Barra crofters, who send the raw material to the Orasay factory, and supplies are also obtained from Orkney. The seaweed is dried and milled at the factory, then sent in bags to the main processing and reduction facilities at Girvan, Ayrshire, to produce thickeners, gelling agents, stabilisers and the like for use in the food, textile, paper, pharmaceutical and cosmetic industries. The processes used at Girvan are based on those evolved by E. C. Stanford, who discovered alginic acid in 1883.

Textiles

Both knitting and cloth-making feature in the economic pattern of North Uist, the latter activity stretching back a long way. About 1750 Lady Margaret MacDonald, a daughter of the Earl of Eglinton and wife to Sir Alexander MacDonald, 7th Baronet of Sleat, founded a 'linnen manufactory' on North Uist. At this time flax was grown extensively on the west side of the island, as the name of the township of Knockline (Cnoc-na-Lin) records. Doubtless the factory was in the nature of a cottage industry designed to establish and encourage the erection and use of looms to produce linen. Many such 'manufactories' were set up in the Highlands during the same period.

A more important cottage product was the heavy cloth known today as one of the recognised types of Harris Tweed. While much of the early produce was for domestic use, there is evidence of a surplus being exported. There is the suggestion, too, that mills existed to serve as 'fulling mills', for scouring and thickening the cloth as it came off the loom, a process normally carried out by women at home rather than in the more formal surroundings of a mill.

Under the influence of the various Home Industries bodies which operated in the Highlands and Islands in the second half of the nineteenth century, the production of cloth for export increased. By 1900 there were a number of looms employed in weaving tweeds, blankets and drugget for petticoats. The tweed was of excellent quality and sold for the standard price of about 3s per yard. It was a true 'home' product in that all stages from fleece to finished cloth were carried out by hand. In 1900 a branch of the Duchess of Sutherland's Home Industries Association was opened in Lochmaddy, to encourage the production of Uist tweed. The Duchess also provided good modern looms to replace the older wood-beam machines. The new looms cost £7 10s od, of which sum the Home Industries Association was prepared to pay £3 10s od, leaving the balance to be paid by the weaver in easy instalments. The work of the Association in North Uist was helped by grants of some £300 from the Congested Districts Board. By 1914 the output of tweed which qualified for the stamp of the Harris Tweed Association amounted to about 47,000yd, valued at about £6,600.

The present output of tweed from North Uist is small in comparison with the Lewis output, despite the presence of a spinning mill at Locheport. But the island can lay claim to two weavers who produce a genuine home product: Lachlan MacDonald of Grimsay and Mrs Peggy MacDonald of Locheport. Mr MacDonald has become known for his designs and quality products, which excite the interest of customers in Britain, USA, Canada and in Europe. Mrs MacDonald produces a high quality cloth, performing all the processes herself and making her own dyes from the island's wildflowers.

In 1970 it was announced that a knitwear factory at Bayhead would be set up by Hebridean Knitwear Ltd, with the help of grants and loans from the Highlands and Islands Development Board. The factory aims to employ sixty workers by the end of 1974. It is equipped (like its sister factory on Tiree) with hand flat knitting machines. The company's production is based on a specially designed range of knitted sweaters of distinctive Hebridean design, which have a high sales appeal, particularly in the export market.

The heavy cloth now qualifying for the Harris Tweed 'Orb' mark has always been produced in the Uists for home wear, though it has never quite reached the level of economic importance it holds in Lewis. In South Uist about 500,000yd of cloth were produced in 1959, though a large proportion was not eligible for the 'Orb' mark since it was produced for non-island tweed producers. This production was the output of some eighty weavers. It is much less than this today, however, the market demand for authentic Harris Tweed, woven in any of the Hebridean islands, being concentrated on the Lewis production.

The history of cloth production in South Uist is not well documented. In 1912 the output was some 6,500yd (of 100 per cent handspun cloth) worth about £900, representing only 3 per cent of the total Hebridean output, a proportion which was never greatly exceeded in subsequent decades.

A new era began in 1950, when a mill on the Scottish mainland began to send treadle looms to South Uist. Some were installed in a weaving shed in Lochboisdale, and others were let out to crofters who undertook to perform a minimum amount of weaving. The finished greasy webs were then returned to the mainland mill for finishing. The low selling price of the resultant cloth, marketed as 'Harris Tweed' though not entitled to be stamped with the 'Orb' mark, threatened the main Harris Tweed industry in Lewis. In 1955 the Harris Tweed Association investigated the situation on South Uist, where, apart from a small factory-type building (converted from former tearooms) in Lochboisdale, a much larger depot had been opened at Iochdar in the north, with about sixty looms in a hall and two sheds. At this time about 120 weavers were producing cloth from mainland-spun yarn. In both depots weaving was being carried out under factory conditions and the weavers were treated as employees, though there was a certain latitude regarding working hours. Each weaver produced about two tweeds per week.

The looms were supplied and maintained by the mainland firm, MacDonald's Tweeds, of Oban, whose foremen tuned them and trained the crofters in their operation. Each tweed produced was a little over 40yd long, for which the weaver was paid £8 10s od. There was a monthly bonus of 7s if the weaver produced eight tweeds in the month. In addition to MacDonald's of Oban, other mainland-based firms had begun to take an interest in the Harris Tweed market to launch their own output of cloth. Uist-produced unmarked cloth was taking about 17 per cent of the genuine Harris Tweed market, a matter of serious concern to the Lewis tweed producers, who wished to preserve the authenticity of their product and the fidelity of their mark. In the end the law came down in favour of the genuine cloth. Cloth is still produced at the depot at Iochdar, but the output is not significant. The weavers receive about £6 per tweed and can average about £20 weekly.

Much of the cloth once made on Barra was for local use. The island to some small extent participated in the increased interest in what was to become known as Harris Tweed at the turn of the century. Lady Gordon Cathcart, who owned the island at the time, with South Uist and Benbecula, acted as agent for tweeds produced by her tenants and sent the cloth to London. But the island has never become associated to any significant degree with the wealth and economic stability which the Harris Tweed industry has brought to the island of Lewis.

As an example of the occasional pocket of private enterprise on Benbecula one might mention the tweed interest of Mac-

Gillivray. This enterprise has been built up from small beginnings, and now sends its tweeds to all parts of the world. The proximity of the airport at Balinavich has undoubtedly been an important factor in the firm's speedy filling of orders.

2   NORTH UIST

NORTH UIST is the largest island in the Southern Hebrides. For the most part it is a low-lying mass, with a few prominent hills to the east and north-east, flat sandy machair to the west, and with perhaps the most complex pattern of freshwater lochs to be found in the whole of the British Isles. The island is about 13 miles north to south and about 18 miles east to west at its widest northern part. A narrow channel separates it from Benbecula. The northern coast of the island is washed by the waters of the Sound of Harris, a sea channel studded with islands, large and small, islets, rocks and sunken reefs. Virtually all these islands belong to the Parish of Harris, though many lie much closer to North Uist; in fact, the only islands in the Sound which belong to North Uist Parish are Boreray and Lingay.

Geologically, North Uist does not differ materially from Lewis and Harris, being based on Archean Lewisian metamorphics, and the mamillations of the grey gneiss, which shows itself in many places, particularly on the higher ground exposed to erosion by sun and wind.

Evidence of ice erosion and deposition is widespread throughout the island. Geikie, in the late nineteenth century, described how the ice once covered the entire island, then moved away to the west and north-west, as may be seen by the orientation of the long axes of most of the interior loch systems (eg, Loch Fada and Loch Scadavay). Ice Age deposits are confined to low ground, the till being described by Geikie as 'a hard gritty and sandy clay, containing much comminuted gneissic material . . . in many places however, it can hardly be called a clay, but is rather a sandy or clayey grit'.

The highest peak, in the south-east of the island, is Eaval, which stands 1,139ft above sea level and is almost completely surrounded by water. Farther north, between Loch Maddy and Loch Eport, rise the twin heights of North Lee (821ft) and South Lee (898ft). All these rises are angular, bare and isolated, in sharp contrast to the rounded ridge series to the north-west and, in particular, to the island's smallest 'ben'—Beinn a' Bhaile—which rises a presumptuous 72ft just south of Balranald.

MacCulloch estimated that the various lochs on North Uist made up at least one-third of the total area of the island. Loch Maddy is a fantasy of inlets, bays, narrows and channels, with a coastline estimated at between 44 and 54 miles in length. Loch Eport, farther south, is a narrow arm of the sea, 7 miles long, which cuts so far inland that only $\frac{1}{4}$ mile separates its head waters from Loch Oban a' Chlachain and prevents the creation of a separate island. The entrance to Loch Eport is almost like a canal cutting, only some 60yd across but running for about 1,200yd, though its depth varies from 7 to 15 fathoms.

Loch Scadavay is the most important freshwater loch on the island; it is shallow and has a calculated shoreline of some 50 miles. It contains about 130 countable islands, though one claim is for a total of 365, a figure probably chosen to agree with the number of days in the year. Loch Obisary, which almost surrounds Eaval on the landward side, has a maximum depth of 151ft. The small loch, Oban nam Fiadh, near the head of Loch Eport is unusual because its waters are partly fresh and partly saline, a characteristic which produces clear distinctions between the species of fauna in it.

The rivers on North Uist are more numerous to the north-west of the island, where they tend to drain water from the ridge of small peaks between Marrogh and Carra Crom, to flow

Page 53   (above) A fleet of herring drifters sail past Kiessimul Castle, Barra, c 1900; (below) more modern fishing boats at Castlebay

Page 54 c 1890:
(*above*) the
Creagorry Post
Office, Benbecula;
(*right*) crofting
scene, South Uist;
(*below*) eviction
scene, North Uist

north, west and south. The drainage pattern of the centre of the island is impossible to resolve, though the origins of one or two isolated rivers present no such problems.

Off the west coast of North Uist lie the two tidal islands of Kirkibost and Baleshare. These are separated from the main island by low sandy shallows, with narrow but deep ebb-tide channels. Baleshare is about $3\frac{1}{2}$ miles long, comparatively level, and connected to Claddach-baleshare on North Uist by a causeway. In its time it has had its share of sand-drifting. In July 1859 much damage was done by high winds, which destroyed crops of potatoes and barley, washed soil away in some places and formed new channels. The southern tip of the island is a marshy depression, but the north end is a remnant of a more extensive machair area washed away from the east side of the island. The western coastline is in constant danger from the Atlantic Ocean, and at Ceardach Ruadh sand cliffs have retreated so rapidly that a stone structure of Iron Age vintage, which has been exposed, will most likely disappear completely within the next decade.

Kirkibost is about $1\frac{1}{2}$ miles long and is approached from Claddach-kirkibost on North Uist. It too has suffered in the past from encroachments by the ocean, and is similar in most other respects to Baleshare. The coastal dunes are particularly high on the south side, while those on the west are deeply serrated by active blowouts. Smooth fertile machair occurs south of a central marshy depression. The 1837 *Statistical Account* records: 'This island was at one time of considerable value. It is composed of the fine sand already described, and being exposed to the western gales a great part of it was literally blown away, and the sea now occupies fields which formerly produced fine crops of bear or barley.'

FAUNA

With South Uist and Benbecula, North Uist affords a safe home

NORTH UIST AND BENBECULA

and breeding ground for many species of birds, particularly water birds. The tangle of lochs on the island offers an alternative breeding area for the greylag goose to Loch Druidibeg on South Uist. The coot is fairly common here among a host of other species that are increasing their numbers—herons, whooper swans, and ducks—a possible reaction to man's encroachment on their traditional breeding and foraging territories on the mainland. Many of the lochs are brackish, which adds to the variety of flora and fauna found around them. Trout are plentiful and afford good sport. A particularly fine species of cockle (*M. baltica*) is also found in North Uist.

Recently a new 1,500 acre reserve was established by the Royal Society for the Protection of Birds, in the Balranald area. One breeding bird of special interest is the red-necked phalarope, whose only other British nesting grounds are the Inner Hebrides, Orkney and Shetland. The reserve was set up by an agreement with the landowners and crofters, and comprises a wide variety of typically Hebridean habitats, ranging from Atlantic beaches with sweeping white sands backed by dunes to large stretches of meadow land (machair), with an abundance of wildflowers, and a variety of lochs.

Included in the reserve is Hougharry township. The fact that the local pattern of land use has changed little over the years is seen in the large number of corncrakes and corn buntings which frequent the reserve, in contrast with other parts of Britain where changes in harvesting methods have driven these species away.

The small offshore island of Causamul forms part of the reserve, acting as a breeding station for a small number of Atlantic seals and as a natural refuge for much of the winter population of surface-feeding duck. The most important loch for waterfowl is Loch nam Feithean, which has large areas of bog. There is an RSPB warden at Hougharry, and visitors are asked to contact him if they wish to enter the reserve.

The Atlantic grey seal is found on a few islands in the Sound of Harris, on the Heisker Rocks off the west coast of the island, and around Grimsay and Ronay to the south-east. These animals are protected by a special Act of Parliament, which was invoked in 1921, when two North Uist crofters attacked some seals and were brought to the notice of the Procurator Fiscal, though no further action was taken.

Herds of red deer on North Uist keep mainly to the uplands, though occasionally the animals come down on to the lower slopes to forage, and cause road accidents at night.

A long-eared bat was sighted at Balranald in 1904, flying around farm buildings and hawking around some dwarf alders. On the shore at Tigharry stands Slochd a' Choire (Kettle Spout), a natural rock arch and spouting cave, near which are other caves wherein breed numerous flocks of pigeons.

PREHISTORY

North Uist abounds with the evidence of its ancient past. Three items worth noting are the Neolithic pottery kilns at Eilean-an-Tighe, the chambered cairns of Clettraval and Unival, and the wheelhouses.

Eilean-an-Tighe is a rocky islet in Loch nan Geireann. Excavation has revealed what may prove to be the oldest recorded example in Western Europe of a potter's workshop. So many potsherds and wasters were found that nothing less than a pottery manufactury could have existed here, to supply the needs of the inhabitants of North Uist and the neighbouring islands. The pottery is of high quality and the patterns show great variety and artistry. The foundations exposed indicated a pit and a couple of kilns.

Clettraval is at the centre of the north-western corner of North Uist. There is a chambered cairn, or passage grave, which seems to have been erected at a time when there was no peat on North Uist, but rather an abundance of birchwood copses, since charcoal derived from birch was found within the burial chamber. Later, during the Iron Age, a fort (one of 100 or so visible forts in North Uist, most of which are on islets) was built partly over the cairn. Much of the Neolithic earthenware found on the site came from Eilean-an-Tighe.

On the west shore of Loch Huna, on the slopes of Unival, there is another chambered cairn, this one having a small cist adjoining the chamber. When the site was being investigated, careful observation enabled the excavators to work out the ritual procedure followed in successive funerals. To the south of the site lies Barpa Langass, a large cairn about 72ft in diameter and about 18ft high. It is a chieftain's tomb, dating from about 1000 BC, whose north side has a small tunnel entrance leading to a cell. The whole structure is an impressive sight as one comes upon it from across the moor. There are a number of these 'barps' in North Uist.

Wheelhouses are to be found at Machair Leathain and Udal, the former being the more impressive. These structures are discussed more fully in Chapter 4 under the Kilpheder wheelhouse (see p 100).

EARLY HISTORY

Of later date, and of no less interest, are the ecclesiastical structures in North Uist, one of which—Teampulla na Trionaid (Trinity Temple)—is of the greatest importance. The ruin stands on the summit of a knoll on the Carinish promontory. It dates from the early twelfth century and is supposed to have been founded by Bethog (daughter of Somerled, the progenitor of the Clan Donald), who was the first prioress of Iona from c 1203. The thirteenth century saw the rebuilding and enlargement of the structure by Prioress Beatrice and later by Amie MacRuairidh, who was a chieftainess at the time of Robert Bruce. She married John, Lord of the Isles. In 1560, after the Reformation, the church fell into disuse, but in its time it was recognised as an important site in the Outer Isles and was for many decades a centre for the training of priests; in fact it has been claimed as the oldest university in Scotland. It was near this church that the Battle of Carinish took place in 1601, the last battle to be fought in Scotland solely with swords and bows and arrows.

Feith na Fala, the Field of Blood, is the name of the battle-field. The cause of the battle was a feud between the MacDonalds of Sleat and North Uist and the MacLeods of Harris and Dunvegan. The feud reached boiling point when Donald Gorm Mor MacDonald divorced his wife, Mary MacLeod, and sent her home. To avenge this insult about sixty MacLeod men took boat for North Uist to lay waste the island. They arrived at Teampulla na Trionaid 'to tak a prey of goods out of the precinct of the church at Kiltrynad wher the people had put all ther goods and cattal, as in a sanctuarie'. They were met by sixteen good North Uist MacDonalds who literally chopped the MacLeods to pieces in a stiff fight, only two of the latter escaping. A third, Donald Glas MacLeod, attempted to escape but was caught and, tradition has it, hit on the head and killed; he was subsequently buried at Teampulla na Trionaid, and in 1840 a skull with a gash in it was reported as 'lying about in the church'. The other dead MacLeods were buried where they fell at Cnoc Mhic Dho'uill Ghlais (Hillock of Donald Glas) beside the shore.

The church ruins are in need of care and attention. Though the site has been considered of sufficient merit to be classified by the Scottish Development Department as a first-category building of historical interest, urgent measures are needed if it is not to become little more than a hump of rubble surrounded by ancient tombstones. Constantly battered by wind and rain, the structure has deteriorated more in the past decade than in the previous 100 years, despite appeals from the North Uist District Council. Archaeological interests have paid scant attention to the abundant evidence of Scotland's ancient past as it exists on the west coast and in the Hebrides compared with that paid to the Roman occupation of Scotland. In their defence it might be said that lack of funds, in comparison with those made available to archaeological interests in England and Wales, have hampered the work of investigating, for instance, the period AD 1000–1500, which included the period of the Lordship of the Isles.

RECORDED HISTORY

In common with the other islands of the Outer Hebrides, North Uist displays in its placenames evidence of the Norse period of occupation. After the defeat of King Haakon at Largs in 1263, the island's fortunes became closely associated with the Norse/Celtic families who ruled it during the twelfth and subsequent centuries. Historically, North Uist was an important part of the territories of MacDonald of Sleat until the late nineteenth century; the territories were divided into two, Clan Donald North comprising Skye and North Uist, and Clan Donald South (or Clan Uisdean) comprising Islay and Kintyre. The MacDonalds were descendants of the Lords of the Isles, who had acquired the island from the MacRuairidhs (sometimes spelled McRurie) of Garmoran (the lands comprising Moidart, Arisaig, Morar and Knoydart on the Scottish mainland). The MacRuairidh family held North Uist for nearly a century. When this sept of MacGorrie (from Godfrey, a son of John of Islay, first Lord of the Isles) fell into decay with the death of John MacGorrie, they became tenants of the Clan Uisdean in parts of the lands on the island which had been ruled by their predecessors.

John of Islay was the great-grandson of Amie MacRuairidh, who rebuilt Trinity Temple at Carinish. There is a Royal Charter of James IV (10 November 1495, 2 years after the Lordship of the Isles was forfeited) which confirms Hugh MacDonald of Sleat's title to the lands of North Uist. Tradition has it that although this Hugh (or Uisdean) had his seat at

Dunsgaith in Skye, he was buried in Sand in North Uist, c 1498. After this date there was a short turbulent period during which Hugh's sons (six in all, and by as many mothers) claimed and counter-claimed the Clan Uisdean lands. Thereafter a period of relative stability ensued.

In 1716, on account of support given by Sir Donald Mac-Donald to the Jacobite Earl of Mar, the lands were forfeited. They were offered for sale in 1723, and bought by Kenneth MacKenzie, an Edinburgh lawyer acting on behalf of the Sleat family, for £21,000 sterling. This transaction was followed in 1726 by a contract of sale between MacKenzie and Sir Alexander MacDonald, a minor who, in the following year, received a Crown Charter of his lands 'erecting the whole into a Barony to be called the Barony of MacDonald'. A subsequent descendant was created Baron MacDonald of Sleat by King George III in 1776. The island thus continued in the possession of the same family (lineal descendants of Hugh MacDonald, the founder of Clan Uisdean in 1469) until the year 1855, when it was sold to Sir John Powlett Ord, Bart, who later sold off the estate in fragments. The estate at present belongs to Lord Granville.

ISLAND CLEARANCES

The eviction of people from their homes in North Uist during the last century was a sorry and shabby affair which did no credit to those in authority nor to the proprietor, Lord Mac-Donald of Sleat, who called in troops to quell his rebellious islanders. This example of a chief turning against his people made the situation worse, for in other parts of the Highlands and Islands the clearances were initiated by incomers who had no association with those they evicted from their homes.

The trouble began in 1849, when Lord MacDonald found that the people of Sollas were resisting his measures to re-use his lands, and decided that force was necessary. Towards the end of July, the *Cygnet* sailed from Skye with thirty-three constables and Lord MacDonald's commissioner, Patrick Cooper, on board. On 1 August this force marched from Lochmaddy to Sollas, where a large crowd had gathered. Talks were held between the two sides and, as the day drew to a close, two men were arrested as 'ringleaders'. The talks had only strengthened the resolution of the crofters to hold on to what little they had. Contrary to a report in the *Inverness Advertiser* that they 'had sent a petition to Lord MacDonald praying for assistance to emigrate', the crofters had in fact said: '. . . If Lord MacDonald would only increase the crofts to double the present size, for which there is improvable land, and would give leases and encouragement to improvements, we would be content to pay rents, and we would have seaware and stock sufficient.'

On the following day the police decided that talking had got them nowhere and that they would have to carry out their orders. Under the personal supervision of Cooper, the force descended on the nearby township of Malaclete, where the Sheriff Officers had asked each of the inhabitants in turn whether they were willing to emigrate. In each case the answer had been no. The constables forced their way into each house and dragged out the tenants' few belongings—sticks of furniture, clothing, bedding. Divots and thatch were ripped from the roof and the timbers of the houses flung into a heap ready for firing. As they carried out their work, a woman rushed from her house to say that her children were being murdered. The watching crowd of crofters were suddenly inspired to action and began to gather stones to do battle with the police. Thus began one of the bloodiest incidents in the period of the evictions in Inverness-shire and the Islands.

In the end the batons of the police got the upper hand of the crowd, mostly women, who retired, many with serious injuries. The legal representatives then tried to introduce a lull in the proceedings by pointing out that the writs of removal were incompetent: they did not correctly designate the houses to be removed, the names of the occupants were incorrectly spelled, initials were used instead of full names, and so on. After this, it was decided that only a token removal should take place. This was carried out, again amid scenes of violence which gradually lessened. The Church of Scotland minister, the Rev MacDonald, told the crofters that provided they would sign an assurance that they would emigrate in the following spring, they would be allowed to remain in their homes during the coming winter. His pleas, interspersed with threats of hellfire and brimstone, were eventually accepted. He was not, in fact, the people's pastor, for they were members of the Free Church; but their own minister, the Rev MacRae, was, strangely enough, absent throughout the whole affair.

At Locheport, too, evictions were carried out with no less severity.

> . . . The lands which they (the crofters) had held were fertile, and there they had lived prosperously in ease and plenty . . . Many were compelled to emigrate to the colonies, and in one ship conveying them, fever broke out, to which many succumbed. Others who remained in the island got corners in other places, while the remainder were supplied with labour by the Highland Committee . . . The houses were knocked down about their ears, and they got no compensation for anything on the ground . . . The severities of the winter, living in rude turf huts, and without fuel, except what they had to carry twelve miles, told on the health of many. The place . . . was overcrowded where they now lived, there being thirty crofts, on which forty families lived, where formerly there were only three.

In the early years of this century the farms of Sollas and Grenetote were divided up by the proprietor into a total of thirty-two holdings, and improvements were paid for by the Congested Districts Board. A total of £1,312 was lent to the settlers for housebuilding, and by 1912 they had paid up all annuities due and there were no arrears, thus justifying their humane treatment.

POPULATION

The average age of the population of North Uist has been increasing since the beginning of this century, and there is at present an excess of males over females on the island. The island reached its maximum population in 1821 with 4,971 persons, since when there has been a steady decline to the 1969 estimate of 1,835 persons. The effect of the clearances is seen in the nineteenth-century figures. Many islanders left for America between 1771 and 1775, again in 1828, and in the period 1841–2. The causes included the depressed price of kelp, the continued state of insecurity, the lack of opportunities for innovation and improvements, and the total failure of the potato crop in 1846.

The figures for the North Uist population in Table 1 have been rounded off to the nearest hundred:

TABLE 1   *Population of North Uist*

Date	Population	Date	Population	Date	Population
1755	1,900	1851	3,900	1921	3,200
1764	2,200	1861	4,000	1931	2,800
1801	3,000	1871	4,100	1951	2,200
1811	3,800	1881	4,300	1961	1,900
1821	5,000	1891	4,200	1971	1,850
1831	4,600	1901	3,900		
1841	4,400	1911	3,700		

RELIGION

In common with South Uist and Barra, North Uist was once Roman Catholic, and before that the old Celtic Church held sway over the island. Tradition gives credit to St Adamnan, the biographer of St Columba, for the island's conversion from paganism. The new broom did not sweep entirely clean, however, and for many centuries an honest acceptance of Nature in the scheme of things was a matter of course. St

Michael, the great saint of both Uists, was remembered each year on Michaelmas Day, 29 September. On this feast day it was common practice to 'borrow a horse to ride for St Michael', a custom which persisted in Protestant North Uist until 1866, when it was practised on Traigh Mhoire (Mary's Strand) on the west of the island, though by that time its religious significance had diminished considerably.

In 1792 the islanders were all of the established religion except 'four of the Romish persuasion'. In 1837 the records show the island again to be all Presbyterian, with the exception of two Episcopalian families and two individual Catholics. The Disruption of 1843 led to the formation of a large Free Church congregation. After the passing of the Declaratory Act a considerable number joined the Free Presbyterian Church or the 'Seceders'. Later, the union of the Free Church with the United Presbyterian Church led to a further disruption, after which some people went in with the union, while others adhered to the old Free Church.

North Uist today is a Presbyterian community mainly adhering to the established Church of Scotland. Having suffered many decades of neglect and depression, and insecure both in land tenure and in hopes for the future, the islanders translated the 1843 Disruption almost greedily into real terms, as people did elsewhere in the Highlands and Islands. Many who had been starved of the necessary spiritual solace provided by communion with a church to which they truly belonged (it must be remembered that many of the clearances which took place throughout the Highlands and Islands were effectively helped by the ministers of the established church) immediately grasped at the new faith and corpus of belief as a revelation.

The great evangelical movement of the Free Church after the Disruption filled a great gap in men's lives. The innately religious people responded with an almost fanatical enthusiasm, which still exists today in some Highland communities. While the bulk of the Free Church following today is to be found in the north and north-west of Scotland (Lewis has some of the Church's largest congregations), there is a strong following in North Uist.

The Church of Scotland, the Free Church of Scotland and the Free Presbyterian Church are all represented in the island. Services are normally conducted in Gaelic, with the occasional service in English during the summer for the convenience of tourists.

CROFTING

Martin Martin, writing towards the end of the seventeenth century, says of North Uist:

> The Cattle produced here, are Horses, Cows, Sheeps and Hogs, generally of a low stature . . . Their Cows are also in the Fields in the Spring, and their Beef is sweet and tender as any can be; they live upon Sea-ware in the Winter and Spring, and are Fatned by it, nor are they slaughtered before they eat plentifully of it in December. The Natives are accustomed to salt their Beef in a Cows Hide, which keeps it close from Air, and preserves it as well, if not better, than Barrels, and Tasts they say best when this way used: This Beef is transported to Glasgow, a City in the West of Scotland, and from thence (being put into Barrels there) exported to the Indies in good Condition.

Later the *Old Statistical Account for Scotland* mentions that the island supported about 2,000 cows, about 300 of them being exported annually at prices varying from 45s to 55s each. Some 1,600 horses were also kept, but as these were used extensively on the land, relatively few were exported. They were valued between 40s and 120s each. The *Account* reads: 'There are no farms here fit for sheep, but every tenant endeavours to rear as many as will furnish him with a little mutton, and wool for clothing. They never thrive so well as to enable the tenant to export any.' The *Account* also mentions that horses were bought 'in great numbers yearly' from Skye and Lewis.

The *Statistical Account* of 1837 listed the island's produce:

500 small tenants: 4 cows each or 2000 at average 15s per cow ... £1500
Tacksmen in all about 300 cows each at £3 ... £900
3000 bolls of grain at 16s ... £2400
Potatoes & etc: 50,400 barrels at 2s ... £5040
Sheep, including all kinds ... £400
Hay ... £200
TOTAL = £10,440

The produce, however, tended to vary as the years were either good or bad. Meal, for instance, had often to be imported, while cattle and horses appeared in export lists. Potatoes had been introduced into the Uists around 1743, and became so plentiful during the following half-century that they formed the principal food for about 5 months in each year—when there was no blight, as occurred in 1846.

The passing of the Crofters Act in 1886 marked the beginning of a prosperous period, in which crofters were given reasonable incentives to improve their land and stock. The North Uist crofters have done just this. Today there are about 460 crofts on the island, most of them far larger than those in other crofting counties, and capable of supporting a man and his family without their having to find an ancillary occupation to supplement their income.

Land on North Uist tends to be used principally for the raising of store cattle, and crofters participate in the Uist Calf Scheme (p 114). But it was also hoped that the prosperity of the island could be increased by a new activity—bulb-growing. In 1956 the West of Scotland Agricultural College initiated a pilot scheme to demonstrate the climatic and other advantages of the machair areas of the west for growing bulbs. Sporadic interest led to some small-scale experiments, but they met with such varied success that doubts were expressed about the whole concept. After the Highlands and Islands Development Board was set up, attention was drawn to the areas of machair in the north and north-west of North Uist, and intensive investigation by the Board's staff and soil experts from the Netherlands resulted in 6 acres of bulbs being planted in 1967 on land sublet from crofters. The bulbs were lifted in the following year and most varieties showed considerably increased yields, particularly those which grew well in the Netherlands. In 1968 a further 20 acres were planted, and each year since then has seen an increase in the acreage under bulbs. The whole project has reached the stage at which, given expert management, large-scale but concentrated bulb-growing could be a profitable undertaking.

To this end a Dutch firm was commissioned to investigate the possibility of reclaiming an area of 1,500 acres of tidal calcareous sands known as the Vallay Strand. The final report confirmed the technical feasibility of such a scheme, and the H & I Board asked the Secretary of State for Scotland for authority to proceed with the reclamation. The request, made in 1969, was turned down in 1972, so the present 'Little Holland' comprises no more than 50 acres at Balmore.

FISHING

The association of North Uist with fishing extends back over three centuries to the fishery schemes of Charles I. For at least 100 years after that time Lochmaddy was an important centre for herring fishing. Before the year 1640 'The Company of the General Fishing of Great Britain and Ireland' (which received a Royal Charter in 1632) built storehouses on a small island (Faihore, which Martin refers to as Nonsuch) in Loch Maddy, and also on Hermetray, an island at the north-eastern tip of North Uist. The company met with strong opposition from the inhabitants of the Western Isles, a conflict of interests which forced it to choose smaller islands for its curing stations and storehouses. Martin, writing of Lochmaddy, remarks: 'The

Natives told me that in the Memory of some yet alive, there had been 400 Sail Loaded in it with Herrings at one Season; but it is not now frequented for Fishing.' When and how the company ceased fishing is not known, unless it was one of the effects of the Civil War in England.

Not until the middle of the eighteenth century was interest in herring fishing again aroused. This time, as before, the island men who participated in the industry tended to be employees rather than entrepreneurs. Though a number of them had boats, these were small and more suited for inshore fishing (for white fish and shellfish) than for use in deeper waters. Between 1881 and 1902 the number of herring boats based on Uist was five, while the number of boats engaged in white and lobster fishing rose from fifty-six in 1881 to a peak of 113 in 1886, then fell to forty-one in 1902. The value of the catch increased, however: in 1889, with 101 boats, the shellfish catch was valued at £1,155, but in 1902, with forty-one boats, it was valued at £6,610.

Today the island's fishermen concentrate on lobsters. The lobster grounds off the west coast of the Outer Hebrides are considered among the best, if not the best, in the British Isles. In recent years, with the introduction of large diesel-engined boats, the areas fished have been extended so that the whole of the west coasts of North and South Uist are fished extensively; large boats regularly fish up to the 20 fathom mark. No fishing of any importance takes place off the east coast of the islands, because the sea bottom is generally muddy and is not suitable for lobsters.

Although the industry has always been able to catch fish, it has suffered in the past from an inability to market its catch adequately. In the early days the fault lay in the lack of suitable fast transport to mainland markets, which often resulted in many thousands of lobsters dying before they reached their destinations. Later, use was made of air transport, but this was expensive and was unable to cope with large catches. Even so,

Page 71 c 1890:
(above) crofting
scene, North Uist;
(left) typical
house, South Uist;
(below) the market
at Ormaclett,
South Uist

Page 72　(above) Benbecula, looking south over the South Ford towards the hills of South Uist (Peter's Port Road); (below) South Uist scene, near Loch Carnan

the Continental market for lobsters was particularly attractive. French and Belgian customers used their own chartered aircraft to fly out consignments of about 5,000lb per shipment. The flights took place once or twice per week from Benbecula airport, in addition to the regular air shipments to the London market.

The first attempt to collect, hold and despatch lobsters to markets under controlled conditions was made in 1967 by Minch Shellfish Ltd (formerly Atlantic Seafoods). In 1968, with the encouragement of the Highlands and Islands Development Board, the present lobster storehouse was built at Grimsay Island, its cost, with ancillary equipment, amounting to some £20,000. The effect of this new storage capacity was felt in that same year, it being the best financially the fishermen had had for years. Landings have increased considerably, from 50,000lb (value £20,000) in 1966 to 129,661lb (value £50,539) in 1968. About fifty boats (from Barra, South Uist, and North Uist, and Mallaig) participate in the fishing, about 75 per cent of the landings being made by boats from North Uist. The Grimsay storehouse has four full-time and nine part-time employees.

As fishing was such an important element in North Uist's economy, and one on which families representing about 500 people depended solely for their living, it came as a blow when the military authorities announced in 1969 that they were extending their rocket range in the western sea areas. Before 1969 the military use of the sea area south of the Sound of Monach was minimal; though regular test firings had taken place, they had occurred so infrequently, and were so spaced, that, either by design or accident, no boat had ever been removed or asked to leave the firing area. But now the fishing areas were to be closed to the lobster fleet, since the boats had to visit them twice a day to set down pots, lift others and re-bait; if a lobster boat cannot reach its fleet of pots daily, at any time during the hours of daylight, the area is said to be unfishable.

E

A public meeting did nothing to help matters, nor did the answer to a Parliamentary question regarding the worth to the islanders of the military presence in the Uists. Some £200,000 per annum, it was said, was paid in wages to civilian employees on the rocket range, a figure claimed to be about five times the annual proceeds of the lobster harvest in the area. In fact the sum paid in wages was nearer £50,000, compared with £75,000 derived annually from the lobster fishing.

The position at present is an uneasy peace, with the military providing a 40ft boat to patrol the lobster grounds to warn fishermen of the times of test firings. But one is left wondering why the testing of obsolescent defence missiles is considered to be of greater importance than the livelihood of a considerable number of islanders.

ROADS

Towards the end of the eighteenth century internal communications in North Uist were poor, but this was probably no particular hardship because, from a contemporary remark, it seems that the island had only eight carts. The islanders walked or rode on horseback and the lack of roads was not greatly felt. Between 1817 and 1837 there was an attempt to improve matters, and by the latter date the island had some 30 miles of good roads, many of them constructed by statute labour and charged to the occupiers of the land. One such was the Malaclete–Dusary road, about 4 miles long and called the 'Committee Road' on account of its origin as a public relief work during the potato famine of 1846. Grimsay Island had the distinction of having a road, about 2 miles long, maintained by the road rates; it was built about 1853 by the Destitution Committee.

North Uist is now served by a circular trunk route of about 35 miles which serves most of the townships on the island. Secondary roads lead towards Berneray and to Locheport.

Metalled but untarred roads serve as internal routes within each township area, particularly in the Paible district and on Baleshare Island. A new road scheme for Baleshare, costing over £130,000 (to serve twelve crofts), will put one of the richest agricultural areas in the Western Isles in communication with the main island mass.

While the visitor might accept the island's roads as being adequate, the islanders have strong feelings about the state of repair of their system; one recent description of a bus ride from Lochmaddy to the North Ford was 'like being on a boat heaving in the sea'. The main reason for the seeming neglect by the Local Authority is an archaic rule which is observed by the national road authorities to the effect that there can be no main road in the Western Isles, and so no route can qualify for the same kind of attention as is given to routes on the British mainland.

TELECOMMUNICATIONS AND POSTS

In 1837 'At Lochmaddy there was, for many years, a Post-office, under the name of Carinish: it is now converted into a sub-office to Dunvegan (Skye). It is difficult to assign any good reason for this. From Lochmaddy, a packet of 60 tons burthen sails, when the weather permits, twice a week to Dunvegan, the nearest safe harbour in Skye. Letters and papers are received at this place, in the surprisingly short time of four days from Edinburgh. This packet is supported by an assessment, which bears heavily on all classes of inhabitants, together with a small sum allowed by the Post-office.' Although Lochmaddy was North Uist's main receiving and dispatch centre for communications, it was not until 1881 that it received official recognition in the form of Post Office facilities, along with Bayhead, Carinish, Locheport, Sollas and Tigharry. In 1903 it seems that letters were able to reach North Uist from Edinburgh in 2 days at the most—a letter posted in Edinburgh before 8 pm would be in Lochmaddy on the following night. Not so today, however. At present first-class mail arrives and departs daily, through Lochmaddy. Second-class mail and parcels arrive and leave by steamer on Mondays, Wednesdays and Fridays. There are twelve post offices on the island.

The first telegraph office in North Uist was established at Lochmaddy in 1880, and by 1886 a telegraph cable had been laid between Lochmaddy and Rodel in Harris. But it was not until March 1946 that Lochmaddy was recorded officially in the 'List of Exchanges'. There are at present about 200 ordinary subscribers on the island, supplemented by twenty call offices. Grimsay Island has sixteen ordinary subscribers and two call offices, a reflection, perhaps, of the importance which this small island has in the economy of the Uists.

LOCHMADDY

Though prominent in the affairs of North Uist today, Lochmaddy was not always a synonym for the island. The first notice of Lochmaddy in documentary records appeared in 1616, in a complaint of piracy and murder in Lewis which makes a special mention of 'Lochmaldie on the coast of Uist' as being a rendezvous for pirates. Later, when the English commercial fishing interests were centred on Loch Maddy, the village was said to be in strong opposition to the activities of the Company of the General Fishing of Great Britain and Ireland. In 1695 Martin Martin records: '. . . the Seamen divide the Harbour in two parts, calling the South-side Loch-Maddy, and the North-side Loch-Partan. There is one Island in the South Loch which for its Commodiousness is by the English called Nonsuch.'

In the nineteenth century, with the increase in communications and the boom in herring fishing, the port came into its own and has remained ever since the capital of the island. Lochmaddy was also important as being one of the 'market' centres of the Uists, along with Ormaclett (South Uist) and

Benbecula. These Markets or Fair Days were socially and economically important.

The present population of Lochmaddy is just over 300. There are the usual facilities befitting a 'capital', including the cottage hospital, hotel, bank, courthouse, prison, shops, County Council buildings and the post office. The pier was built during the ownership of Sir John Ord. Originally it consisted of a concrete embankment with a wooden structure of greenheart piles covered by a wooden decking, plus a general waiting room and mail and cargo stores. In 1948 the pier was sold to Inverness County Council, which, through the agency of the Department of Agriculture for Scotland, completed its reconstruction in 1955. More recently cattle pens to accommodate over 300 head of cattle have been added to the existing facilities, and over 2,000 are exported through Lochmaddy each year, with a similar number of sheep. General cargo is landed by small coasters, including bulk goods such as coal, bricks, sand, road chips, fencing stobs, fertiliser and Calor gas. The vehicle ferries from Skye (which now carry commercial vehicles) have increased traffic fivefold since the service was introduced in 1964.

ISLAND LIFE

Perhaps it is because the island has a rich potential, yet to be fully exploited, that North Uist presents such an air of confidence in the future. These are, of course, hard times for islands, so when one finds an island community alert and fully aware of its own ability to carry the present and future generations into the coming decades, one hopes that central authority will not lay a leaden hand upon it. 'Conservation' is admirable, but an island community also includes human beings; it may well be that those who at present seek to retain unspoiled areas as national parks should remember the human element in their desire to conserve the natural environment and the lower species.

There is a tendency among outsiders to use the word 'dying' when talking or writing about the Hebrides. There is also the use of the word 'depopulation', which seems to imply that a death knell is sounding. But the islands are not dying, and though they may be underpopulated, they are in fact beginning to retain the number of people they can support at a tolerable level of living. Overpopulation has always resulted in scratching for subsistence, and islanders will no longer tolerate this.

There are many signs of new life on North Uist, most of these deriving from the three activities involving alginates, shellfish and bulbs, which give employment to and absorb part of the population. Though the ratio of old to young is still high, this is not so bad a sign as first appears, because the old people in the Hebrides tend to live independently and purposefully for longer than elsewhere. Young people are, however, returning to the island, and it is in some ways encouraging to know that in North Uist there are six people waiting for each piece of land that falls vacant.

There are of course social and economic problems. But, unlike those found in grossly overweight conurbations, they are scaled down to community size, where individuals can effectively participate in their solution.

The proprietor, Lord Granville, is the exception rather than the rule among Highland landlords. He has encouraged enterprise on his estate and has acted as both entrepreneur and catalyst. Recently he had a consignment of seedling oysters flown in from a research laboratory in England, to produce what could become the first generation of a new species of Hebridean shellfish. Fish-farming has been encouraged, to restock and revitalise the island's lochs. Innovation has been introduced in the shape of two catamarans for lobster and prawn fishing, and these craft have proved their worth in Hebridean waters. Perhaps it is a sign of the times that the familiar craft of the New Hebrides in the Pacific are playing a part in the economy of the old Hebrides.

In common with other Hebridean islands there is the problem of maintaining Gaelic-based cultural values. But there are signs of a new awakening to the fact that the islanders' identity is firmly attached to their language and, provided that there is no overwhelming influx of outsiders into the island, the present decline could well be halted and reversed. The 'x-factor' in island-living is the effect of remote decisions taken by textbook planners and administrators for the Hebrides; but given that these are sympathetic, there is no reason to doubt that life in North Uist and its neighbours will be as vigorous and as valid by the end of the present century as it is today.

3   BENBECULA

THE island of Benbecula (Beinn a' bh-faodhla—the Mountain of the Fords) is the flattest island in the Outer Hebridean chain—an area of bright, green and fertile machair, and of bogland. The highest point on the island is the peak of Rueval (408ft). The western coastline looks to the Atlantic with a smooth low-lying face of sandy beaches. On the eastern side there are deeply indented sea lochs and a maze of small islands and island rocks. It is roughly rectangular in shape, about 6 miles one way by 8 miles the other. John McCulloch said of it: 'The sea here is all islands, and the land all lakes. That which is not rock is sand; and that which is not mud is bog; that which is not bog is lake; that which is not lake is sea; and the whole is a labyrinth of islands, peninsulas, promontories, bays and channels.'

The interior of the island is full of small lochs, many of whose tiny green islets support the ruins of ancient duns or forts. These lochs provide very fine trout fishing and are havens for many species of birds, both resident and migrant. The western part of the island possesses the bulk of Benbecula's crofting and grazing land, with its characteristic linear township settlements; and these are connected by good surfaced roads.

The island is famed for its population of snipe, duck, geese and swans, and many species of seabird are also to be seen. The moorland supports such birds as the songthrush, stonechat, meadow pipit, golden plover, and hedgesparrow. Eagles, redshanks and some other species rare 10 years ago have now become plentiful. Native mammals include the vole, pigmy shrew, fieldmouse, and the rabbit, the last named flourishing on the sandy machair land but rarely appearing on the moorland.

The island supports a variety of wild flora, each species being located in its characteristic environment—seashore, machair, dry moorland, marsh, exposed land-rises and, on the eastern side, cliff faces washed regularly by the spray from the Minch waters. Supporting as it does a typical Hebridean flora, the island's insect life is no less interesting.

The island of Wiay (which rightly belongs to the parish of North Uist, but lies closer to the mass of Benbecula to the south-east) is a bird sanctuary.

Benbecula has always attracted the sportsman, a species which has, however, never been made quite so welcome as the birds. C. V. A. Peel found this out at the turn of the century:

Much of the pleasure of shooting in the Outer Hebrides is spoilt by the conduct of the crofters. It is not conducive to sport to be followed by a gang of men and ordered out of the country, nor is it pleasant to be cursed in Gaelic by a crowd of irate old women, even if you do not understand every word they say. They accused us of shooting their horses and sheep, filled in the pits which we dug in the sandhills for geese, shouted to put up the geese we were stalking, cut up the canvas and broke the seats of our folding-boat, and tried in every possible way to spoil our sport.

Though Benbecula is known in Gaelic as the 'Mountain of the Fords', the only 'mountain' is Rueval, which stands about $1\frac{1}{2}$ miles east of the main north–south road. A drove road runs from the main road at the old Market Stance towards Rueval, which is merely a rounded hill with grass and heather slopes, but has a splendid view from the top. MacCulloch made the climb and attempted to count all the lochs he could see: 'For a time the count went on well enough. Great and small, crooked and round, and long, and serpentine, I arrived at thirty, and forty, and fifty, and sixty, and then I was obliged to adopt a new plan, and thus I got up to seventy. At eighty they began to dance before my eyes; but at length, in spite of all my contrivances my head began to whirl, and at the ninetieth I gave up the point in despair.'

Benbecula once belonged to the MacDonalds of Clanranald. In 1839 it was bought for £40,000 by Lt-Col John Gordon of Cluny in Aberdeenshire. He died in 1858 and was succeeded by his son, also John Gordon, who in turn was succeeded by his widow, later Lady Gordon Cathcart. She died in 1935 and the island estate was administered by Trustees who sold the northern part of Benbecula to the Air Ministry in 1942 and the bulk of the island to Herman Andrae, a London banker in 1944.

The MacDonalds of Clanranald, descended from the Lords of the Isles, were an old-established family in South Uist and Benbecula, and featured in many Gaelic songs and traditions. Their seat was at Ormaclett in South Uist, but when that building was burned down in 1715, the family moved to Nunton in Benbecula and lived there until the connection with their estates came to an end in 1839. Nunton was the home farm attached to Borve Castle, an important seat of the family, situated at the south-west corner of the island. The house of Nunton still exists as a farmhouse; despite alterations and additions, the older parts can be clearly recognised. Nunton was once the site of a nunnery, which fell into ruins, and its stone was used in building the new farm. Nearby stands a small ruined chapel in an old burying ground.

Borve Castle, or what is left of it, is one of the major secular buildings surviving from the Middle Ages in the Outer Isles.

It is said to have been built in the fourteenth century by Lady Amie of the Isles, and may be the structure referred to in a document of 1373 as the 'Castle of Vynvaule' (Benbecula). Its walls are built of random rubble set in thick mortar, and are 9ft thick. It was occupied up to about 1625, Ranald MacDonald of Benbecula then being alluded to as 'of Castell-brof'. The castle had at least three storeys. It is curious that Martin Martin, usually most observant, fails to mention Borve Castle, though he writes about Nunton.

In 1931 a carved stone ball was found on the nearby seashore; it is thought to have some connection with the remains of an Iron Age site and kitchen midden there. The ball is the only specimen of its kind ever discovered in the Hebrides. These balls usually have six faces, but that found at Borve has four only, and is thought to have been some kind of mace head displayed at warlike ceremonials.

Benbecula has many sites of interest. In Loch nam Meirbh are two small islands, Meirbh Bheag and Meirbh Mhor. In the centre of the former, Little Meirbh, there is a rock with a hole in it which seems to be partially man-made. It is said that criminals were once deposited in this hole, tied to a stake and left to die, the water covering their feet and legs. In due course their remains were carried over to 'Great Meirbh' for burial. Tradition also says that this fact accounts for the beautiful hue of the wild hyacinths which grow there. In Loch Olavat there are no fewer than three duns on small islets. Another interesting place is Dun Bhuidhe, Yellow Fort, on Loch Dun Mhurchaidh to the north-west of the Market Stance.

POPULATION

While virtually all other islands in the Hebrides are experiencing a decline in their population, Benbecula is one of the few in which the population has increased—through the influx of military personnel and their families. Before 1958, when the rocket range at Iochdar on South Uist was first begun, the downward trend after the middle of the last century, and a gradual ageing of the population, were features common to other Hebridean islands. In 1764 the population was about 600. The next recording occurred in 1841, with a population of 2,107. Thereafter the figures (to the nearest hundred) are those shown in Table 2.

TABLE 2 *Population of Benbecula*

Date	Population	Date	Population	Date	Population
1851	1,700	1881	1,700	1931	1,000
1861	1,500	1891	1,500	1951	700
1871	1,600	1901	1,400	1961	1,300

Included in the 1961 figure were 34 persons who were wholly Gaelic-speaking and 821 who were bilingual. This left 457 persons who were wholly English-speaking, virtually all of them connected directly or indirectly with the rocket base, some 30 per cent of the whole. The 1971 population census figure is expected to reveal an increase (to about 60 per cent) in the numbers of incomers to Benbecula, with a serious decline in that sector, generally containing those over 60 years of age, who are wholly Gaelic-speaking.

RELIGION

Benbecula has been described, with some dramatic intent, as a buffer zone between two religions—Protestant in North Uist and Catholic in South Uist. Benbecula is almost equally divided between the two. One leaves South Uist for Benbecula with a real sense of merging, but road shrines gradually decrease as one travels north from Creagorry. While there has been no actual attempt at ecumenism, the two communities are extremely tolerant towards each other, and in fact the religious division of the island has caused fewer problems than has the more recent confrontation between the Gaelic-speaking community and the military personnel.

The religious scene was quite different, however, two centuries ago. A Captain Below of the Buffs, stationed in the Outer Hebrides, then wrote of Benbecula:

> The Inhabitants are all bigotted Papists, and frequently make their Boasts to the Soldiers when quartered there, of what execution they did against the King's Troops at the Battle of Prestonpans. There is a Presbyterian Missionary resides in this Island but he has a miserable time of it. He set some Men to work with an Intention to build himself a House, but he has never been able to compleat it, for what was built in the Day, was almost demolished in the Night by People Unknown, and the poor man durst not complain for fear a worse Treatment should ensue.

ECONOMIC BASES

With less than seventy crofts, Benbecula's economy depends on building work and the provision of services for Balinavich airport and the rocket range on South Uist. From the experience of other island and remote-mainland communities which have had Government defence projects dropped in their midst, it is doubtful whether, considering how quickly defence plans became obsolete, the community on Benbecula will benefit in the long term from its present prosperity. On the other hand, it can be argued that the presence of the military base represents an opportunity for locals to remain on their island and enjoy a standard of living that could not be got from crofting and fishing. The problem seems now to be more social and cultural than economic. Many of those employed in building would more than likely be on the mainland working in similar employment, with continual pressure for their families to join them. It is certainly better in the short term for them to be able to find work near home.

The ultimate requirement of the military establishment is

85

some 300 houses for its personnel, together with shops and the like to offer normal services to the military community. The nearest chemists' shops, for instance, are at Stornoway on Lewis or Mallaig on the Scottish mainland.

The pattern of crofting on Benbecula follows that on the Uists generally. Fishing is concentrated on shellfish, and in particular lobsters, to supply a demand from an increasing and lucrative market. The existence of the large lobster pound on the island of Grimsay to the north-east of Benbecula has enabled lobster fishermen to withstand the tyranny of a fluctuating mainland and continental market.

The existence of an expanding community creates a demand for specialist services. For instance, in 1970 a qualified television engineer took up residence in North Uist to cover the Uists, Barra and Benbecula. Again, the demand on the public electricity supply has increased and the construction of the new power station at Loch Carnan in South Uist will inevitably create a number of vacancies for skilled and semi-skilled workers.

Tourism has increased in recent years and the island caters for the tourist by offering bed and breakfast accommodation. Caravan sites are being developed. While no estimate exists of the income from this new element in the island economy, there is no doubt that it has increased to the stage where it is considered worthwhile to inject private capital into existing facilities or to create new ones.

ROADS

The road system on Benbecula is concentrated on the western side of the island, the main route running from Creagorry in the south to Gramisdale in the north. Generally following the western coastline is another road which serves to link up, with laterals, the crofting townships and the airport at Balivanich. Footpaths allow travellers to make their wettish way across the eastern side of the island to reach Rossinish, Meanish and Rarnish. From the south end of the main road an eastward lateral runs to Peter's Port, on Eilean na Cille. These roads now carry considerable traffic, both tourist (from the roll-on/roll-off ferries) and military. There is a daily bus service (Sundays excluded) run by Messrs MacBrayne, who took over the services from local operators in 1947. The bus links Balivanich with Lochboisdale in South Uist.

TELECOMMUNICATIONS AND POSTS

In 1872 telegraph cables were laid between Benbecula and its neighbours. In 1904 telephone cables were laid to the island. In 1942 a telephone repeater station was completed, and in March 1946 'Benbecula Exchange' was recorded for the first time in the GPO 'List of Exchanges'. A new telephone exchange and relay station is now being completed.

In the early years the mails were delivered on foot or by horse and trap. The late Donald MacDonald provided his own motor vehicle in the 1930s for the delivery of the mails, and it continued to run until the red Post Office vans were introduced at the end of World War II. Mail arrives at Balivanich (for Nunton PO, opened in 1881) daily by air, and it is also sent out daily. There are other post offices at Creagorry, Gramisdale and Liniclett.

PETER'S PORT

Many tales are told about small places in the Hebrides, and Peter's Port is no exception to the kind of humorous situation that only bureaucracy can provide. Towards the end of the last century there was considerable agitation for a pier to be located roughly midway between Lochmaddy and Lochboisdale. Two rival sites were offered—at Loch Carnan, at the north-east corner of South Uist, and Peter's Port, at the south-east corner of Benbecula under the shadow of Wiay Island. Peter's Port was chosen.

87

The works were completed in 1896 at a cost of £2,000, voted by Parliament under the 1891 Western Highlands and Islands Act (for the construction and improvement of small harbours, piers and boatslips in the crofting counties). The main responsibility for the adoption of such schemes lay with the County Councils, and in the case of Peter's Port versus Loch Carnan the result was a bureaucratic blunder of the first order.

Firstly, access to the site by sea was extremely difficult. Secondly, there were no plans to build roads to the pier, which just jutted out from the countryside. Thirdly, after the pier was completed, a further £100 had to be spent in removing a very large rock from its seaward end; but even with this improvement it was never used as a port of call. Skippers regarded it as dangerous. Captain Osborne Moore of HMS *Research* made a survey of the area and reported: 'The masters of steamships trading and carrying mails in the Hebrides, for whose benefit the pier was constructed, refuse to use it, as they consider it and the approach to it as dangerous. Their objections are reasonably justified.'

The pier, lacking an approach road, existed for some time as a planners' folly in glorious isolation. To remove the error of omission, a further grant of £1,800 was made to construct a good road which, while it brought some crofting townships into touch with the rest of Benbecula, did nothing to enhance the value of Peter's Port as a place of call for ships. In fact, not only had the road to be built, but a causeway was also necessary to link the island on which the pier was sited, Eilean na Cille, with the rest of Benbecula. As late as 1931 the *West Coast Pilot* dryly remarks: '. . . there is neither village nor inhabitants, but a steamer calls occasionally with supplies for the southern side of Benbecula, which are landed and taken away in boats . . . the approach is so difficult, and there is so little room to turn, that it is not used by the local steamers. The port should not be entered without local knowledge.'

Page 89 (above) Traditional thatched house near Sollas, North Uist; (below) the old farmhouse of Nunton, Benbecula

Page 90   Thatched houses at Howmore township, South Uist

ISLAND LIFE

The existence of a large English-speaking community on Benbecula has created some problems for the indigenous Gaelic-
speaking population. In Balivanich, for instance, the natives
are outnumbered by the incomer population by more than
two to one. Both cultural and social problems are looming and
in 1971 a survey was carried out to investigate the effects of
the incoming population on the island. A strong case has been
made out by those who are anxious to see that the cultural
integrity of the island is kept intact. Loss of the Gaelic would
mean loss of the island's identity, a problem faced by small
communities with powerful neighbours throughout history.
Unfortunately for the conservationists more English is being
spoken by island schoolchildren now than ever before. Once
the language of the playground was Gaelic. In 1904, a Schools
Inspector wrote: 'Practically every child . . . speaks Gaelic
and Gaelic only from the time he leaves school in the evening
till the morning on which he returns. The language of the
playground is Gaelic and any communication that is made by
one pupil to another in school is almost always in the same
language.'

One instance, apparently trivial, of the effect of the new-
comers on the island revealed itself in 1971. This was the naming
of streets in the army housing schemes after officers associated
with the rocket range instead of bending slightly to use more
traditional names. The event caused no end of comment and
provoked Comunn na Canain Albannaich (the Scottish
Language Society) to accuse the army on Benbecula of being a
pollutive element in an existing Gaelic culture.

Being a small community, the island has offered only a small
contribution to the corpus of Gaelic language and tradition.
In 1948 a crofter, Angus MacMillan, completed 500 recordings
of folklore and stories, one item lasting for 4 hours. But it is

doubtful if Benbecula will long be numbered among the truly Gaelic-based communities of the Hebrides.

One result of the rapid social and economic progress on the island has been the establishment of a small police force of two locally based constables—this after a period of 20 years with no need for a policeman.

The true character of Benbecula lies not so much in its topographical features or its history as in its indigenous population, which has demonstrated, in its religious harmony, that human relations do not depend on a homogeneous belief but on a simple desire to work together.

4   SOUTH UIST

SOUTH UIST is the second largest island in the Southern Hebrides, being some 22 miles long, north to south, and varying in width from 6 to 8 miles. It is an island with sharp physical contrasts: all along the western side are flat sand-based machair lands about 1 mile in width which support most of the crofting townships and offer good soil for cultivation and for grazing; while the eastern side is wild, with boggy moorland that rises west to east to meet a long spine of high hills running the length of the island. Three long sea lochs—Skiport, Eynort and Boisdale—enter the island from the Minch, dividing it into three distinct parts. Loch Skiport joins Loch Bee to the north-west, all but cutting off the Loch Carnan area. The whole island is threaded through and through with freshwater lochs, many of whose small islets bear the ruins of prehistoric forts or duns. The lochs are well known for their populations of brown trout and wild duck.

There are three groups of hills on South Uist, all confined to the belt of high ground running north and south on the east of the island. The southern group lies between the south end of the island and Loch Boisdale. The highest peak is Easaval (800ft), followed by smaller rises such as Roneval (660ft) and Marava (530ft). The second group lies between Loch Boisdale and Loch Eynort and contains about ten high hills, each distinct, with two exceeding 1,000ft. They are mostly covered with grass or heather and show little bare rock. The highest peak is

Stulaval (1,228ft), followed by Triuirebheinn (1,168ft). Between these two peaks, in Bealach a' Chaolais (Pass of the Narrows), stands a typical example of an earth house, in a good state of preservation, and the remains of several circular stone chambers. The third group contains the principal summits in South Uist and lies between Loch Eynort and Loch Skiport. The group includes Beinn Mhor (2,033ft) and Hecla (1,988ft). Hecla is a fine shaped rise surmounted by a mass of rock, and a grassy ridge leads to Hecla's secondary summit (1,820ft). Just south of the subsidiary peak, Cas fo Thuath (1,154ft), is Glen Corodale, from which a stream empties into Corodale Bay. This is a remote spot in which Prince Charles Edward hid for several weeks during the summer of 1746. There has never been any house at Corodale, though readers of Neil Munro's *Children of the Tempest*, a novel set in Uist, will find that author's licence has allowed him to place one in this spot. Needless to say, the tops of either Beinn Mhor or Hecla give magnificent views, and on a good day freaks of image can throw up the distant hills of Northern Ireland, well over 100 miles to the south.

South Uist is composed almost entirely of Lewisian metamorphics. Intrusions of later age and gneissic bands of different textures and hardness occur to form local ridges and headlands. Over this base or veneer of glacial drift lies, to the east, the peat and standing water areas, and, to the west, the machair sand— hundreds of acres of blown sand, in dunes, plains, sandhills and ridges. Textural and microscopic examinations have revealed that this sand is a highly variable mixture of silicious and calcareous fractions. The calcareous sand is derived from crushed marine shells and other marine organisms which have either arrived continuously on the South Uist beaches over a long period of time, or may represent the legacy of former marine conditions when marine organisms were more abundant on the basic rock platform. The silicious fraction appears to be derived from glacial drift formerly deposited on the rock platform. That

NORTH UIST

MONACH
ISLANDS

SOUND OF MONACH

Grimsay

Ronay

BENBECULA

Wiay

ATLANTIC

Gualann
Hornish Pt
Balgarva
Ardivachar Pt
Ardivachar

South
Ford

Bagh nam Faoileann

L Bee

Geirinish

BEN
TARBERT

Skiport
Ornish

OCEAN

Howmore

L Druidibeg

HECLA
1988'

Stoneybridge

L Fada

GLEN DORCHA

MAOLA
BREAC
939'

GLEN USINISH

Rudha
Hellisdale

ORMACLETT
CASTLE

SOUTH
UIST

BHEINN
MHOR
2034'

GLEN LIADALE

1994'

Rudha
Ardvule

KILDONAN
GLEN
L Kildonan

L Eynort

ARNAVAL
822'

STULAVAL
1227'

L
Stulaval

Stuley

Dalburgh

TRIUIREBHEINN
1168'

Lochboisdale

L Boisdale

Kilpheder

Calvay

Orosay

N Boisdale

MARVA
570'

Rudha na
Hordag

Kilbride
Ludac

RONEVAL
660'

Sound of Eriskay

N

Lingay

Eriskay

0 1 2 3 4 5 miles

Fiaray

Fuday

BARRA

SOUTH UIST

South Uist was glaciated is evidenced by the quantity of drift, most of which is sandy, over much of the low ground. The argument that the non-shell fraction of the machair sand is derived from glacial deposits is strengthened by the absence of rivers flowing into the Atlantic. Only the Howmore River is of any size and, as several lochs in its path act as sediment traps, little material is carried down to the sea.

THE MACHAIR

The outstanding characteristics of the machair are its low altitude and flatness; the sandhills rarely exceed 30ft in height. Centuries of rainfall, strong winds from all directions, soil creep, grazing and cultivation, have all acted to level the land. Erosive factors introduced by man and his animals, and the inevitable rabbit, have also contributed to the changing scene.

There have been many kinds of investigation into the age of the machair. Among the earliest evidence are layers of wind-blown sand contained in compressed organic deposits, which are found below highwater mark at certain places along the coast. One of these sites, at Borve in Benbecula, yielded some wood fragments dated to c 5800 BC. Archaeological sites have also produced evidence used in dating.

At the Kilpheder site, for instance, excavated in 1952 to reveal the now famous wheelhouse, evidence pointed to the period c AD 100–200. This and other wheelhouse structures are set on or in an older sand surface and have been covered at a later period by severe sand drifting. A Viking house uncovered some 6ft beneath the landward part of Drimore gives proof of further considerable sand drifting since the ninth century.

The sum of the archaeological evidence indicates that over the past 2,000 years or so the machair, or large areas of it, has been covered with a stabilised vegetation suitable for farming. There have been periods of severe sand drifting, but whether these affected the machair as a whole, or only limited areas, as is the case today, is not known for certain.

One of the earliest references to 'machair' occurs in the placename 'Mackermeanache', mentioned by Dean Monro in 1549 and identified as the present-day Eochar. MacFarlane's *Geographical Collections* (1907) has the following description of the Uists based on notes taken in 1630: 'Ancient men of this country say . . . that sand doth flow with the wind, and destroys both the lands, and hides the houses under the sand, and so that the most part of the country is overwhelmed with sand.' Similar descriptions can be found in the literature of succeeding centuries in Martin (1695), Anderson (1785), the *Statistical Accounts* (1794 and 1840), MacDonald (1811), MacCulloch (1824), and Buchanan (1883). All these refer to the existence of the machair—at one time 'fruitful in corn' and excellent for grazing, and at other times consisting of large areas subject to erosion and destruction by sand movements.

The Clanranald Papers also provide similar evidence from 1688 when there is a reference to a machair rental. In a document of 1758 relating to the tack of the lands of Askernish, Garryheillie, Daliburgh and Kilpheder, a clause states: '. . . they must endeavour to stop the encroachment of sand drift and protect the land from foreign waters'. The most detailed description and evidence of the machair surface is contained in the Factor's Reports, written during the 1820s. Throughout the history of this interesting area of land, which is largely similar to that found in other parts of the Outer Hebrides, there is proof of over-grazing and over-cultivation laying bare extensive tracts, with consequent erosion. This state of affairs continued until the present century. Now the land has become reasonably stabilised, and can be described as a vegetation-covered coastal sand-plain whose composition permits the existence of a healthy and prosperous crofting community, not one whose continuation hangs on the whims and caprices of an unstable land surface.

Being so varied in topographical detail, South Uist supports a wide range of flora and fauna, the former including few trees and shrubs and the latter concentrated on birds rather than on animals.

Loch Druidibeg, and the environs of Stilligarry, form a nature reserve, created in 1957. It is largely owned by the Nature Conservancy, which has a resident warden at Stilligarry. The reserve, totalling 4,158 acres, comprises two sharply contrasting areas of land. The eastern section, including Loch Druidibeg, of about 2,500 acres, has an indented shoreline, with many islands and peninsulas, and lies on a bedrock of ancient Lewisian gneiss surrounded by barren heathery moorland. The western section is loch-studded, fertile and grassy—part cultivated machair and part marshy plain. Several of the Loch Druidibeg islands, owing to their isolation from fire and grazing, are covered with a relic scrub woodland of birch, rowan, willow, juniper, bramble and wild rose. Much of the Uist moorland was covered with such scrub at one time. Under these low trees spreads a dense cover of herbs and ferns, with the royal fern dominating.

The greylag goose (*Anser anser*) breeds in this area, one of the few left to it in the British Isles. In winter large groups gather here, and in spring they pair off to nest on isolated sites on the islets of Loch Druidibeg. Immigrant white-fronted and barnacle geese also share the winter haunt. The black-throated and red-throated diver, golden eagle, hen harrier and red-necked phalarope are among the rare birds seen at this reserve.

Loch Ardvule, near Bornish, is another interesting loch which, situated as it is on the promontory of Rubha Ardvule beside the remains of a fort (Dun Vulan, Iron Age to early medieval in date), contains brackish water and supports many species of waterfowl. This area has unusual but attractive scenery.

Running south into Loch Eynort, the Allt Volagir collects water from a number of mountain streams on the way. Nearby is Arinambane, an old ruined house which was once the Inn of South Uist. The river valley is not too difficult to get to, but requires a full day's outing. It is a miniature woodland, mainly of the birch-hazel type, with bluebells and wood sorrel, aspens, sallows, rowans, junipers, honeysuckle and brambles. From cliff crevices cascades of ivy, bearberry, and fern run down the slopes to the rough edges of the river, which tumbles down from Beinn Mhor. In other river gorges, between Lochs Eynort and Boisdale, are found common bugle, agrimony, woundwort, and tuberous-rooted bitter vetch. All these plants are evidence of the woodlands that covered so much of the Western Isles about 2,500 years ago.

On the slopes of the Beinn Mhor/Feith-bhealach/Hecla massif, which rises between Lochs Eynort and Skiport, many northern and alpine plants are to be found, together with some rare grasses and sedges. The mountain gorges harbour a rich and rare variety of ferns, including the delicate filmy fern.

On the flatter machair the usual crop of wild plants occurs, including the ubiquitous primrose, which carpets the area, ragwort, daisies and buttercups. Waterlilies are found in the freshwater lochs, usually waxen-white, but sometimes in the rarer yellow variety, particularly in the area around Loch Minish.

Much work has been done in the past 30 years or so to confirm the fauna of the Hebrides and to prove the existence of geographical races or sub-species.

PREHISTORY AND ANCIENT STRUCTURES

The ancient remains of South Uist include cairns, wheelhouses, duns, brochs, and standing stones. There is a long and interesting trail of evidence to suggest that the human occupation of the island goes back some 3,000 years, though there is a sug-

99

gestion that the climatic changes which occurred about 600 BC made the Outer Isles generally uninhabitable until the first century AD, when the wheelhouse dwellers appeared. The suggestion is contained in the writings of classical authors— the sixth-century AD *Ravenna Cosmography* (in which 'Erimen', a western island whose name is derived from the Greek word for desert, is claimed to be the Long Island), and Plutarch's *De Defectu Oraculorum*, written about AD 120. One must also consider the rarity of Roman objects of early date found in the Hebrides, in sharp contrast with the frequency with which they have been found on the Scottish mainland.

The wheelhouses are drystone-built structures with a most distinctive form. Some are free-standing, with a well built outer wall of earth faced with stone, up to 8ft thick. Others have a much less substantial wall, being built in pits dug in sand dunes. Both forms have an inner diameter of between 20 and 40ft. In the centre of the house is a square or horseshoe-shaped hearth, made from large flat slabs and outlined by stones placed on end in the ground to make an enclosure for the fire. This type of house received its name from the thick stone piers built radially like the spokes of a wheel that divide the space near the wall into eight or more compartments. The piers end at some distance from the hearth, which represents the hub. There the family could sit and follow their various domestic occupations. Evidence as to how the buildings were roofed is scanty. There is the suggestion that the wheelhouse as a form of dwelling evolved from the broch. Such wheelhouses were inhabited during the Roman Occupation of southern Britain. Roman coins and pottery found in them have been useful in dating, but it is difficult to know how many decades to allow for such items finding their way to Scotland. A fourth-century coin found in one wheelhouse suggests that these buildings had a long life.

Two examples of the wheelhouse in South Uist are to be found at Kilpheder and Drimore (the type is also to be found in North Uist, Benbecula, Orkney and Shetland). The Kilpheder example (as yet inexplicably unlisted as an Ancient Monument) is still standing to a higher level than many others. The artifacts found suggest that the wheelhouse dwellers had a simple economy—farming, hunting and fishing. Pigs, sheep and shorthorn cattle were kept and grain was cultivated.

There are many ancient structures to see in South Uist, not a few of which have inevitable religious associations. An Carra is a standing stone to the west of Loch an Athain, near Stoneybridge. This monolith is of regular width for more than half its height of 17ft, and then it tapers towards the top. A barp, or chambered cairn, lies to the south of Loch Ath Ruaidh. It is almost circular, measuring some 78ft from north to south and about 73ft from east to west, and is about 12 ft high. A short length of the entrance passage, nearly 3ft wide, can be traced, and two erect slabs are visible on the south side.

Only the east gable ruins remain of Caibeal Dhiarmaid church, Howmore, which was once dedicated to St Columba. On the north side of the window is a corbel, probably for an altar, and on the south side is a small recess. Caibeal nan Sagairt, Howmore, is an oblong chapel whose gables are steeply pitched and complete but whose side walls are in ruins. Traces of a window remain in the south wall. Another church in this interesting Howmore group is Teampull Mor, once dedicated to St Mary. It was 66ft long and 26ft wide, but all that is left now is the east gable and the foundations of other walls. The circular remains of an earth house, Uamh Iosal, show an external diameter of 26ft. Only the northern part of the building is discernible, the larger southern part of the structure appearing as a mass of loose stones. There are a number of ruined shielings in the vicinity.

HISTORICAL REMAINS

The castle on Calvay Island at the mouth of Loch Boisdale dates from the thirteenth century. Its walls are 5ft thick. At

the south-west corner is a small strong tower containing a
dungeon, and on the north side was the hall-house with a
postern. Some traces of battlements remain. Prince Charles
Edward hid in the ruin for some nights in June 1746.

Ormaclett Castle is a ruin of an unfortified house of the early
eighteenth century, once the home of the MacDonalds of
Clanranald. The builder was Allan MacDonald, who fell
mortally wounded at the Battle of Sheriffmuir in 1715. In his
youth he had been a fugitive from Cromwell and took refuge
in France, but after the Restoration he returned to South
Uist. Later he employed a French architect and masons to
build Ormaclett. It took 7 years to build, and 7 years later it
was burnt to the ground on, tradition has it, the eve of the
Battle of Sheriffmuir.

At Milton can be seen the remains of Flora MacDonald's
house, now merely the drystone walls of an L-shaped dwelling.
A cairn in the centre of the enclosure was raised to her memory
by Clan Donald.

HISTORY

The last quarter of the first millenium AD was dominated by the
Norsemen, in the Hebrides as in much of Western Europe.
Their dominance lasted until the middle of the eleventh century.
Commonly known as Vikings (from the Old Norse *vik*, meaning
bay or inlet), the Norsemen were variously described as pirates,
traders and settlers. They subjugated the settlements they found
on their exploratory visits to the Hebrides and established their
own characteristic type of social organisation. The leaders of
the Norse settlements were the jarls or earls who owed allegiance to the King of Norway. Beneath them was a class of
farmers who were freeholders, not mere tenants; they took an
active part in the organisation of their communities. Each
district had a Thing, which was a gathering of free men to dis-
cuss matters of general interest, to put the law into effect, and
to pronounce judgements. There was also a slave class, derived

most likely from subjugated peoples. It was during the Norse-dominated era that many of the Highland clans originated, including the Clan Donald, the largest Highland clan and one of the most distinguished in Scotland's history. It was under the Clan Donald, as manifested in the old Lords of the Isles, that a Gaelic polity existed in Scotland. Had it continued as a political entity, it might well have moved the centre of Scottish power from the Lowlands to the Western Isles.

Somerled, a Gall-Gael of mixed Pictish and Norse extraction, was the first Regules of the Isles. His father was Gille Bhridhde who, according to tradition, was descended from Conn of the Hundred Battles, High King of Ireland about AD 125. Somerled, as Thane of Argyll, was in frequent conflict with Malcom IV, King of Scotland. Matters came to a head in 1164, when Somerled, with a fleet of 155 ships, sailed up the Clyde and landed at Renfrew, where an army under the Stewart of Scotland waited to oppose him. But Somerled and his son, Gille Calum, were assassinated by Maurice MacNeil, a relative of Somerled's who had been bribed by the Scottish court. Dispirited with the loss of their leader, the Islesmen withdrew from the impending fight.

Somerled was married to Ragnhildis, daughter of Olav the Black, King of Mannin (Isle of Man), and had three sons—Donald, Reginald and Angus. Being of Norse descent, directly from their mother's side, Somerled's sons greatly enhanced their position during the Norse occupation of the Western Isles. This occupation was, however, a great source of irritation to the Scottish monarchy. Alexander II tried to negotiate their cession with King Haakon of Norway, but had no success. His son, Alexander III, was no luckier when he attacked some of the less well defended islands of the Inner Hebrides, for the barbarous treatment suffered by the people of these islands so infuriated King Haakon that he set sail for Scotland in 1263 with a powerful fleet.

Haakon was fully prepared for battle, but Alexander, knowing that he had little chance against the Norse military might, proposed negotiations. Haakon agreed, and Alexander then played a waiting game. He waited for the autumn gales to dislodge his enemy. Too late the Norse King realised that there was no possibility of any agreement with the Scottish King. He prepared to land an army at Largs, but on the night of 30 September 1263 a fierce gale devastated most of his fleet, and the land engagement was little more than a skirmish. Haakon withdrew what was left of his fleet and sailed for Kirkwall in Orkney, where he died of fever two months later. Magnus, the Norse King of Mannin, died in 1266 and created the opportunity for the cession by Norway to Scotland of the Western Isles and Mannin for 4,000 Scots merks plus a yearly rental of 100 merks. Although Norway thus renounced her territorial rights in the Hebrides, the Norsemen left behind them, in various families, a sense of allegiance to a power other than the Scottish Crown. By the end of the thirteenth century, in fact, the Lord of the Isles wielded so much power that Edward I of England looked more to the western seaboard of Scotland than to the Edinburgh of the Scottish King for the ruling power in Gaelic Scotland.

In the War of Independence that led up to the Battle of Bannockburn (1314) Alexander, Lord of the Isles, did not support Robert Bruce, though he did not fight against him. On the other hand, his younger brother, Angus Og, sheltered Bruce when the latter was a fugitive at Dunavery and later fought for him at Bannockburn. Bruce's words before the battle —'My hope is constant in thee'—became the motto of Mac-Donald of Clanranald.

The Lordship of the Isles was forfeited in 1493 on the death of John, 2nd Lord of the Isles, and annexed to the Scottish Crown in the reign of James IV to prevent any future Lord rebelling against the Crown. Various chiefs who had held their lands from the Lordship were offered Crown Charters instead, and almost without exception they made their submission to James.

In subsequent decades, sometimes through the blundering of the Privy Council in Edinburgh, various branches of the Clan Donald combined to revive the Lordship. But the title was never to regain the position it once had. The present heir apparent to the British throne, Prince Charles, has, among other titles, that of Lord of the Isles.

The Clan Ranald of Garmoran is descended from Ranald, son of John, 1st Lord of the Isles, and Amie, the heiress of the MacRuairidhs. Among their possessions were the Uists and Benbecula of the Outer Hebrides. To the MacDonalds of Benbecula, one of a number of cadet branches of Clanranald, belonged two of the most distinguished members of Clan Donald. One was Flora MacDonald and the other Alexander MacDonald (Alasdair Mac Mhaighistir Alasdair), one of the greatest of modern Highland poets. The son of a clergyman, he became a schoolteacher and a master of the Gaelic language. His longest work, a description of a voyage by the galley of Clanranald called 'Blessing of the Ship', has been described as the finest sea-poem written in Britain.

Flora MacDonald was the daughter of Ronald MacDonald of Milton near Mingary. He was a cadet of Clanranald and died when Flora was a year old. Her mother's second husband was Captain Hugh MacDonald of Ormadale in Skye. It was he who, while being in command of a body of militia in Uist, furnished his stepdaughter with a pass for herself, 'Betty Burke' and the boat crew who were to pass the Minch to Skye. Flora MacDonald was at Milton, keeping house for her brother, when she received word of the Prince's plight. And it was in her brother's shieling at Alisary, on the slopes of Sheaval, that she met the Prince. At first she refused her help, for fear that the family would suffer. In her journal she wrote that she 'had (with some difficulty) agreed to undertake the dangerous enterprise'. While she is often presented as a keen Jacobite, in fact it is more than likely she was merely lukewarm to the cause; it is even possible that she was for King George II, since her stepfather was at the time commanding the King's troops in the district and the man she loved and later married, young Allan MacDonald of Kingsburgh, was himself serving as an officer in the King's forces. It was his family that Flora was to place in peril of death—to save a man she did not know and for whose cause she had no great enthusiasm. But with her aid the Prince escaped from Scotland to pursue a career which subsequently, and perhaps strangely, has done little to diminish the romantic aura surrounding the 1745 Rising.

Another famous person connected with South Uist was Jacques Etienne Joseph Alexandre MacDonald, Duke of Taranto, one of Napoleon's marshals. His father, who lived at Howmore, was named Neil MacEachan, but he changed his name to Mac-Donald. His Jacobite interests forced him to flee to France with Bonnie Prince Charlie after the Prince's defeat at Culloden, and his son was born at Sedan. In 1826 the Marshal paid a visit to Howmore, whence he took back with him to France a boxful of the ancestral soil. It is in his grave at Courcelles-le-Roi.

The end for the Clanranald family in the Uists began in 1794, when the Chief succeeded as a minor to estates which paid him £25,000 per annum in rents and which had been in his family's possession for five centuries. But by 1827, after 30 odd years devoted to high living in London and representing an English rotten borough in Parliament, he found himself on the verge of bankruptcy. His agents were obliged to wring every penny piece out of the estates. Various projects were put forward with a view to increasing revenue, one being to develop the kelp industry at a time when the kelp market had been completely undermined by the reduction in the import duty on salt. But efforts were to no avail. The island of Canna was sold in 1828, Eigg shortly afterwards, South Uist in 1837 and Benbecula in 1839. South Uist went for £84,229 to Lt-Col John Gordon of Cluny in Aberdeenshire. Thus came to an end the direct association of Clanranald with the Uists. South Uist now

Page 107 Gathering seaweed for manuring the land. Early spring, South Uist

Page 108 (above) In South Uist, some harvesting is still done entirely by hand; (below) near Lochboisdale, South Uist

belongs to the Earl of Granville and a Glasgow-based syndicate (which also owns Lochboisdale Hotel).

The hereditary bards and historians of the Clanranalds were the MacVurichs, now called Curries. The ruins of their house, which was comparatively large, can still be seen at Stilligarry. The MacVurichs kept commonplace books in which items of clan history, anecdotes, genealogical information, panegyrics and elegies for their own and other chiefs were entered. These records were written in classical Gaelic, which was the common literary language of Ireland and the Scottish Highlands and Islands down to the beginning of the eighteenth century. The MacVurichs were in fact the last practitioners of Gaelic bardic verse anywhere. Their 'Red Book of Clanranald' has been published, with a passable translation, in *Reliquiae Celticae.*

ISLAND CLEARANCES

In common with the other Hebridean islands and the mainland of north Scotland, the clearing of people from estates in South Uist by the agents of the proprietors was accompanied with much cruelty and inhumanity. In 1849 and 1851, upwards of 2,000 persons were forcibly shipped from South Uist and Barra to Quebec. Some were induced to embark voluntarily under promise that they were to be conveyed free of all expense to Upper Canada, where, on arrival, Government agents would give them work and grant them land. These conditions were not fulfilled. They were turned adrift at Quebec and thence compelled to beg their way to Upper Canada. The Canadian papers teemed with accounts of the miseries endured by these unfortunate Highland emigrants, whose misfortunes were aggravated by the fact that they could speak only Gaelic, so that they were practically strangers in a foreign land (see also p 135).

THE UISTS AND BARRA

South Uist's population was at its highest between 1836 and 1846. As in North Uist, there has been from 1951 an excess of males over females, which has varied from about 2 to 10 per cent. The population has remained steady during the past decade at about 2,400. The average age is much less than North Uist's, however, and the population's rate of reproduction most likely reflects the ability of a Catholic community to offset the serious effects of youthful emigration which has been the experience of other non-Catholic islands. The South Uist population figures (to the nearest hundred) are shown in Table 3.

TABLE 3   *Population of South Uist*

Date	Population	Date	Population	Date	Population
1755	2,200	1861	3,400	1931	3,300
1801	4,600	1871	4,200	1951	3,100
1811	4,800	1881	3,800	1961	2,400
1821	6,000	1891	4,300	1966	2,400
1831	6,900	1901	4,100	1969	2,400
1841	7,300	1911	3,800		(estimate)
1851	6,200	1921	3,600		

Various census returns have illustrated the decline of Gaelic. According to the *New Statistical Account for Scotland* (*Invernessshire*) in 1837, there were only about a dozen people in the Uists who did not understand Gaelic. The first census enumerating the Gaelic-speaking population of Scotland was that of 1881, but then there was no distinction made between those who spoke 'Gaelic only' and those who spoke both 'Gaelic and Engligh'. In South Uist then, of a population of 3,800, only 236 persons did not habitually speak Gaelic. In 1891 a distinction was drawn for the first time between those who spoke Gaelic only and those who were conversant with both languages, and in that year about 60 per cent of the total fell in the 'Gaelic only' category. By 1901 this percentage had decreased to 53. Today only about 100 people speak Gaelic only, though about 80 per cent are bilingual.

RELIGION

With Barra, South Uist has remained faithful to the Catholic religion, despite social and economic pressures that could have weakened and changed the beliefs of the islanders. In the year 1758 the south end of the island, together with Eriskay, was disponed by the young Clanranald to Alexander MacDonald, a kinsman and a son of Donald MacDonald of Benbecula. This Alexander took the territorial title of 'Boisdale'. In 1770 he renounced the faith of his ancestors to become a Protestant with all the zeal of a new convert, and proceeded to take tyrannical measures to compel his tenants to follow his example.

He used to drive them to Church with his thin yellow cane, so that the Protestant Church in Uist became widely known as the 'religion of the yellow stick'. He also called a meeting of his tenants at which he read out to them a paper in Gaelic ordering them to renounce the Roman Catholic faith and never again have any business with their priests. They were then called on to sign the document as a condition of their continuing to retain their holdings. If they failed to comply, they would be summarily removed. The tenants, however, held fast and refused to sign. The whole affair was bruited abroad, to the concern of many prominent British Catholics, lay and clerical alike. As a consequence, MacDonald of Glenaladale on the Inverness-shire mainland, who had interested himself in the dilemma of the South Uist tenants, bought an estate in Prince Edward Island in Canada and emigrated there with 200 persons, of whom 100 were from the Boisdale estate.

The island has, however, never been wholly Catholic: in 1792 about 85 per cent of the population was Catholic, in

1837 75 per cent, and today around 80 per cent. A comment of 1837 says: '. . . the people are quiet and peaceable, and sectarianism has not obtained any footing among them. Those of the Established Church live on the best of terms with their Catholic neighbours.' And so they do today, with a harmony that could well be emulated with effect by other communities where the two religions exist in a spirit of determined disunity.

The chapel at Bornish was originally erected there because that was the centre of the South Uist population, but the centre has now shifted farther south and the building stands isolated as a monument to its own past. It is a quiet building, built of natural island rock, with the inside walls left quite bare. Two other chapels are St Peter's at Daliburgh and the newer church at Garrynamonie. This latter building is an angular structure of striking design. A mosaic on an external wall, designed and executed by David Harding, depicts our Lady of Sorrows accompanied at the Crucifixion by Mary Magdalene and St John. The scene of the crucifixion and the two crosses of the thieves are merely suggested. To the left, at the top, are sharp jagged red thorns symbolising pain and suffering, and on the right are the instruments of the crucifixion—two hammers, three nails and a scourge. The sun and moon traditionally symbolise the attendance of the whole universe at the crucifixion, the shape formed by areas made from pebble suggests the hill of Calvary, and another area of jagged pieces of slate is a device used to lend an ethereal atmosphere to the whole scene. The colours are sombre and low-keyed, fitting to both the theme of the mural and its island setting. The materials used are local, as are those used for the Stations of the Cross inside the building —slates from Eilean Stolaidh (Stuley Island on the west coast of South Uist).

Another visible sign of the island's role as the heart of the Catholic Hebrides is the tall slender statue of Our Lady of the Isles and the Holy Child which stands on the side of Rueval, about 4 miles south of Carnan. Designed by the sculptor Hew

Lorimer and erected by the people of Iochdar parish, it over-
looks the rocket range on Iochdar and out to the waters of the
Atlantic, beyond which, legend has it, lies Tir nan Og, the
Land of Youth and the Isles of the Blessed.

CROFTING

South Uist has always been fertile, and its old-established
tradition of exporting is exemplified in the following extract from
the *New Statistical Account for Scotland* (1845).

7719 bolls of bere, oats and rye at £1 per boll—	£7719
82,760 barrels of potatoes at 2s per barrel—	£8276
10 acres turnip at £11—	£110
23,000 stones of meadow hay, at 6d per stone—	£575
1000 stones of cultivated hay, at 8d per stone—	£33
1600 cattle at an average of £3—	£4800
400 pigs at 10s	£200
Eggs sent to Glasgow, at 2s 6d per 100	£625
25 tons cod and ling fish, at £20 per ton—	£500
1570 tons of kelp at £3—	£4710
TOTAL value of yearly raw produce—£27,548	

Crofting on the island today still tends to be more prosperous
than it is in many other parts of the Highlands and Islands,
though the fertile machair on the west has at times been over-
exploited in the past. The island is famous for its cattle. Sheep
are also raised, but they are confined to the steep and hilly
pasturage on the east of the island.

There are about 750 crofts, a number which is declining
slowly and represents a decrease of some 150 on the 1966
figure. The decrease, however, is accounted for mainly by the
amalgamation of crofts to form larger and more economical
units. The existence of the rocket range, (which offers full- and
part-time employment), fishing for shellfish, seaweed collection,
and general construction work have all helped to stabilise the
population, and few crofts are left vacant because their owners

have been forced to emigrate by pressure of unfavourable economic circumstances.

The number of stock reared on South Uist justifies local sales that attract auctioneers from the Scottish mainland. A new scheme by which calves are sold and taken to mainland farms for intensive rearing, the Uist Calf Scheme, has received capital grants from the Highlands and Islands Development Board. The idea behind the scheme is to improve the marketing and breeding of cattle in the Uists, and it is run by Hebridean Calf Producers Ltd, a cooperative based on Lochboisdale, and formed by the Scottish Agricultural Society Ltd to carry on a scheme of calf marketing which it had been operating previously. The crofter gets paid for his beasts by Hebridean Calf Producers Ltd on the spot at the Lochmaddy sales, and the calves are then fattened on mainland farms through the winter months, a more economic proposition than wintering the beasts in the islands. After the animals have been sold, any profit made by the cooperative is distributed among the crofters who originally sold the calves. On the breeding side, research is being carried out to improve the calf strain. The Development Board has also provided non-economic grants to build cattle pens and a weighbridge at Lochmaddy.

Ponies were once a common export from South Uist, the sales of these animals being held at Lochboisdale. The ponies have now largely gone from the island scene, their tasks being taken over by tractor and lorry.

FISHING

Alongside crofting, fishing has been important to South Uist. About a century ago Lochboisdale was an important centre of the Minch herring industry and shared in its prosperity. As with other island ports, however, the indigenous population, through lack of capital, were not able to become principals in the industry. There were nine herring boats in South Uist in

1892, and twenty-nine 10 years later. White fishing reached its peak in 1890, when 171 small boats were operating off the island. Then came a decline to sixty-three boats in 1902, but after years of slackness a gradual increase occurred. In 1938 there were 101 boats (motorboats of under 30ft keel) operating out of Lochboisdale. The catch was mainly herring, though its value (£865) was much less than that from shellfishing (£2,600). After World War II, in 1948, 160 boats produced a herring catch valued at £6,100, compared with shellfish at £4,700.

In more recent years the island's fishermen have benefited from the Fisheries Development Scheme of the Highlands and Islands Development Board, which has resulted in new specially designed boats being made available to suitable applicants. Assistance has also been given by the Board to experienced fishermen in the purchase of good secondhand boats.

There has been a concentration on shellfishing, mainly around the Loch Carnan area. Lobsters are the main harvest, and these have been dealt with already under North Uist (p 70). Eleven boats based on South Uist now work the lobster grounds full-time.

MILITARY EMPLOYMENT

In 1955 the Ministry of Defence proposed that the Iochdar site on South Uist be developed as a rocket-testing range, with a monitoring site on St Kilda. The proposal met with a great deal of opposition, but the inevitable took place: the area to the west of Loch Bee became a military base and a series of changes in the island's economy and social patterns began. In 1968 further plans for the extension of the existing Hebrides Range were announced—to allow particularly unit practice with the new low-level air-defence weapon Rapier, and for the flying of the army's surveillance drones. The ultimate establishment will be in the region of 330 military and 200 civilians, though not all of the latter will be drawn from the island population. We have dealt with the islanders' objections to these plans on p 85.

GENERAL EMPLOYMENT

In South Uist this comprises building work, transport (bus and motor services), tourism, and some minor production of craft objects for tourists to buy. The tourist industry has not become established, though the island is scenically attractive and offers archaeological exploration, hill walking, golf (at Askernish), fishing and bathing. Fishing is a tourist attraction that has much potential. The group of lochs in the Howmore area carries an enormous head of fish. Farther south, the Kildonan water system offers very good sea-trout sport. Loch a' Bharp is a good salmon water. The South Uist Angling Club exists to control brown trout fishing in a number of lochs, and its facilities are made available to visiting anglers. Another tourist attraction, though it performs a more basic social function on the island, is the Uist Games held each July. The piping competitions in particular draw expert pipers from far and wide.

Public works in recent years have included new road construction, and the Kilpheder canal, designed to drain waterlogged crofts in that area.

ROADS

Writing in 1837 the parish minister of South Uist said that there was a good road running the whole length of the parish, kept in good repair by statute labour and commutation money. There were also at that time good roads running from the main road described to Lochboisdale and Loch Skiport.

Today the same main road runs from Pollachar in the south to Iochdar in the north, a trunk road of about 20 miles in length. There are three main laterals—to Lochboisdale from the junction at Daliburgh, to Loch Skiport pier from the junction at Grogarry, and to Loch Carnan pier from a junction near

Ollag. Other roads are classed as minor roads and mainly serve the various townships. Originally the roads were constructed as public works and maintained by farmers and crofters, though not infrequently they were found in bad repair. Ultimately the responsibility for the roads came under the County rate system and they are now well maintained. The Daliburgh–Lochboisdale road was first constructed as a relief measure in the years of the potato famine, 1846–8.

There is no traceable record of the first motor car on South Uist, but there is a description of the first bicycle on the island's roads, at the turn of the century:

> Looking north along the road from my house I saw a strange figure more than a mile away. It was coming along the road too fast for anyone walking yet it was not anyone on horseback. As the object came nearer it dawned on me that it was a man on a bicycle—a strange sight for our island! . . . it was Mac-Queen from the Estate Office . . . I inspected his machine, and I asked him how long he had had it. 'Only a few days', he said, 'but this is the first bicycle ever brought to the island'. . . . He told me that the women were afraid of it, for if they saw him with it they scurried into their houses and quickly shut the doors. But the men made a great tumult about it and had been to the Factor complaining that it frightened the horses and cattle, and they wanted the bicycle banished from the island.

TELECOMMUNICATIONS AND POSTS

In 1837 it was recorded that South Uist had no post office: 'The nearest Post Office is at Lochmaddy in North Uist, about 66 miles distant from the south extremity of the parish.' Post offices were eventually opened in 1881 at Iochdar, Howmore, Daliburgh and Lochboisdale Pier, some of them later becoming telegraph offices. The Grogarry Post Office was opened in 1890. In 1884 a telegraph cable was laid to connect Barra with South Uist, and Eriskay was provided with the same facility in 1902, with Benbecula following in 1904. A wireless telegraphy station is mentioned in the Post Office Records for 1932, but it was not until 1939 that Lochboisdale was recorded in the Post Office 'List of Exchanges'. At present there are over 160 ordinary subscribers, with twenty-two call offices. Statistics were as much the rage 70 years ago as they are now: in a report produced at the turn of the century it was stated that each family in South Uist received an average of nearly seventeen parcels each year.

LOCHBOISDALE

Lochboisdale is a pleasant little sea town (population 316) which consists of a main street, and a few side streets, containing houses and shops. Its lack of formal layout adds much to its atmosphere. There is a bank, hotel, and garage facilities. A small industrial estate is being established. There is also a shop maintained by Highland Home Industries, a concern which echoes the time almost a century ago when destitution was rife in these islands and 'home industries' became the only means of maintaining some kind of living standard for many a poor family.

Occasionally today a big herring catch turns Lochboisdale into a hive of activity. The fishing boats discharge their catches on to larger ships known as 'klondykers', capable of holding some 15,000 crans of herring. The effect of the Skye–Lochmaddy connection across the Minch has, however, considerably diminished the commercial importance of Lochboisdale as a port; and even the number of passengers has decreased, to one-third of the figure of 1962.

ISLAND LIFE

As in other islands, the community on South Uist is closely knit, with all the intangible and some of the physically accessible advantages over most urban societies which such a social structure enjoys. It does not take much insight to realise that the incoming military at the rocket range have brought with them a certain erosive element from which the residual culture, being Gaelic-based, tends to suffer.

Another type of incomer, though less permanent than the army's importations, is the young tourist. It is on record that a West Indian girl who visited the hostel at Howmore said: 'I'm glad "peace on earth" is not mythical or illusory.' The hostel is run by the Gatliff Trust (other Hebridean hostels are at Scarp and Rhenigidale in Harris). The remark tends to mirror the quality of life which exists on South Uist.

It could well happen that the incomer population will attempt to assimilate the ethos which they find in the island and in its neighbours. But where this has been the experience of other areas, the incomers involved were there because of their own decision to find work (eg, in the Lochaber area, attracted by the pulp mill). In South Uist the incomer population is a directed military one, and the military, subject to constant moves, tend to carry their own ethos with them. They will hardly learn Gaelic, and the Gaelic-based culture has no effective way of defending its values. Even the body in Scotland most associated with the preservation of the Gaelic language, An Comunn Gaidhealach, has been strangely silent since its vociferous protests in 1969 when the rocket-firing threatened the lobster fishing of the Uists. Perhaps it has accepted, with a typical Celtic fatalism, the inevitable decrease in the relevance of Gaelic today, even in the Outer Hebrides.

But while the language may decline, some inherent resilience may allow it to outlast the impermanence of military bases and resume some kind of place in the island's society. Much depends on the children of the island, and, in particular, whether economic opportunities allow them to remain on the island to live, work, marry and bring up their own children. The children undoubtedly have the intelligence to appreciate their heritage, and the following comment about South Uist children at the turn of the century is still relevant today:

Without entering upon a comparison between the intellectual capacity of Lowland children and that of Highland children, I am firmly of the opinion that no class of children is more responsive to the stimulus of sound instruction than the Gaelic-speaking children of these islands. As I have said elsewhere, their isolation from the busy haunts of men increases their wonder and curiosity, and for natural shrewdness and sagacity and a capacity for taking on the marks of the higher civilisation they will compare favourably with Lowland children.

There is a growing realisation that the Hebrides are part of the outer and utter fringe of Europe, whose growing economic, social and political integration is creating a hub that may well make already 'remote' areas such as the Scottish island communities remoter still to planners and administrators. It will remain with the islanders to assess just how much they value their inheritance. Only in small societies such as exist in South Uist can a possible remedy be found for the salving of what remains of human values, and this is mainly because these values still exist in the island. Of course, the same can be said of many other small communities whose harshness of existence has made them appreciate the fact that living must always have a sharp edge on it to make it relevant and to give spiritual satisfaction. Members of much larger societies and communities should attempt not merely to preserve such societies for academic dissection, observation and dissertation, but also learn from their values.

5   BARRA

WHEN one approaches Barra from seawards, one receives the first impression of an unfriendly place, bleak, arid and inhospitable. Only when one is close to the coastline does one see that the island is a more welcoming pattern of greens, browns and greys. Barra dominates the southern archipelago between Eriskay to the north-east and Berneray, some 12 miles to the south-west, and is the most westerly inhabited island in Great Britain. It is 35 sq miles in extent, about 8 miles long and about 7 miles wide at its widest. The island is composed of Archean rocks, mainly ortho gneisses, with intrusions of granulites, and traversed by veins of pegmatite. The island, with its southern satellites, was once intensely glaciated by ice moving in a general north-westerly direction, and the result may be seen today in erratics and perched blocks everywhere, with pockets of rubbly drift. There is no true boulder clay.

The island is fairly compact, except for a narrow promontory in the extreme north which is joined to the mainland of Barra by a great cockle beach. The highest peak is Heaval (1,260ft), which rises to the north-east of Castlebay, the island's main township, and affords a magnificent view of the southern tip of the Hebridean island chain. Heaval consists of grassy slopes and rocks which break up its green flanks into a series of slopes and terraces. At the top there is a spine of grey rock which tends to lean towards the south. There are two subsidiary peaks, each over 1,000ft. Heaval is the site of a statue in Carrara marble of the Blessed Virgin and Child, erected during the Marian Year 1954.

Ben Tangaval (1,092ft) at the south-west corner of the island is the only other hill which exceeds 1,000ft in height. To the north are the summits of Ben Eoligarry (338ft), Ben Erival (654ft), Ben Cliad (680ft) and Ben Obe (449ft).

Rich pasture land and meadows spread across the lower levels, but otherwise the island is covered with great stretches of peat moorland. The coastline is varied, from sheltered inlets and the fine harbours at Castlebay and North Bay, to great cliffs and wide sandy bays with huge dunes. Many of the inlets in north-east Barra suggest that erosion along joints in the gneiss, accelerated by prevalent westerly gales, has allowed the sea to invade what were formerly freshwater lochs, now connected to the sea by narrow channels. There are no large rivers on Barra, but water drains along valleys running east and west, and south-east and north-west.

The island's climate is markedly oceanic in character, the annual range in temperature being less than 14° F. March is the coldest month. Rainfall is moderate, between 40 and 50in per annum and well distributed throughout the year, the heaviest rainfall coming in autumn and winter. Strong winds (Beaufort Scale 4 to 7) blow for just over half the time during April and for more than two-thirds of the time in September.

FLORA AND FAUNA

The island carries much of the fauna and flora found elsewhere in the Hebrides. Over 150 species of birds have been recorded. Some are resident species, including the raven, starling, housesparrow, twite (*Acathansis flavirostris bensorum*, a Hebridean native), rock-pipit, songthrush (*Turdus philomelos hebridensis*, another native), blackbird, wren (*Troglodytes troglodytes hebridensis*), merlin, cormorant and, of course, many of the birds of the seashore and cliff.

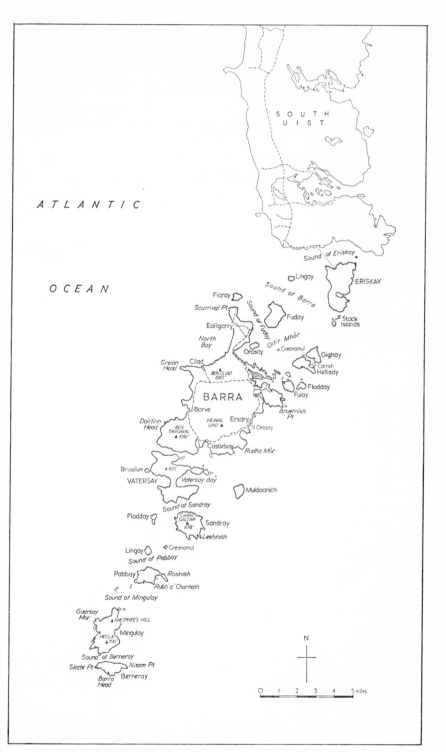

ATLANTIC

OCEAN

SOUTH
UIST

Sound of Eriskay

◌ Lingay

Sound of Barra

ERISKAY

Fiaray ◌

Scurrival Pt.

Fuday

Eoligarry

Sound of Fuday

North
Bay

Stack
Islands

◌ Creanamul

Oitir Mhòr

Gighay

Greian
Head

Cliad

Orosay

Carrish
Hellisay

BEN CLIAD
680'

Flodday

BARRA

Fuiay

Borve

*Bruernish
Pt.*

Doirlinn
Head

HEAVAL
1260'

Ersary

Orosay

BEN
TANGAVAL
1092'

Castlebay

Rudha Mòr

Biruaslum

▲625'

VATERSAY

Vatersay Bay

Muldoanich

Sound of Sandray

Flodday ◌

CAIRN
GALTAR
678'

Sandray

Leehinish

Lingay ◌

◌ Creanamul

Sound of Pabbay

Pabbay

Rosinish

Rubh'a' Charnain

Sound of Mingulay

Guarsay
Mòr

MACPHEE'S HILL

HECLA
700'

Mingulay

Sound of Berneray

Skate Pt.

Nisam Pt.

Berneray

Barra
Head

N

0   1   2   3   4   5 miles

BARRA

The island's mammals include the pigmy shrew, otter, grey seal, rabbit (there is a large warren on the machair at Eoligarry), brown rat, house mouse and Hebridean fieldmouse (*Apodemus hebridensis*).

The flora tends to reflect the maritime character of the island, more than 400 plants having been recorded. Such trees as are found on Barra tend to be stunted and gnarled; they include black poplar, bay willow, alder, common birch, larch, Scots pine, juniper and ash. Masses of primroses transform the machair lands of Barra into a pale yellow sea in springtime, their fragility belying the hardiness demanded of everything that lives on Barra.

About fifteen of the more common and more easily noticeable species of lepidoptera exist on Barra, all of them tending to be of the northern varieties, with the main exceptions of the Large White and the Small Tortoiseshell butterflies.

Fish abound in the coastal waters and include lythe, dogfish, spotted ray, salmon, sea trout, basking shark, eel, and mackerel. Trout are found everywhere in the lochs and streams of the island.

ANTIQUITIES

On the green flank of Ben Eoligarry and looking out across the Sound of Barra is a low squarish wall, a cluster of headstones and a group of small roofless chapels. This is Cille-Bharra, the sacred place of the island. It was the burial place of the Mac-Neils. The dead chiefs and members of their families were taken from Kiessimul by sea in the chief's lymphad or masted galley. The largest of the buildings, the church of St Barr, is simple in design and made from rough stone. The other two buildings are small chapels, once roofed with thatch. Among the grass can be found carved slabs with foliage and interlacing strapwork designs. The only rune-inscribed stone known in the Hebrides was also found hereabouts. It has a cross on one side and a runic inscription on the reverse, and is thought to be a relic

Page 125 (above) Tanks containing graded lobsters at the shellfish plant on Grimsay island, North Uist; (below) drying seaweed at the alginate plant, Orasay, South Uist

Page 126 (*above*) Ferrying cattle across the Sound of Vatersay; (*below*) cattle landing on Barra

of the Norsemen in Barra after they had adopted Christianity in the eleventh century. The rendering of the inscription given by the Norwegian scholar Magnus Olsen is as follows: 'After [ie, in memory of] Thorgerth Steiner's daughter this cross was erected.' The stone is now housed in the Museum of the Society of Antiquaries in Edinburgh.

When Martin Martin visited Barra about 1695 there was a statue of St Barr in the church, a wooden image wearing a linen shirt that was replaced annually on St Barr's Day, 27 September, when there was a great celebration. All the island folk made for Eoligarry, and on arrival they took to horse to ride three times, sunwise, round the chapels. Horse races would then follow on the nearby sands. The 'Barra Account' written for the *New Statistical Account of Scotland*, 1840, talks of '. . . each man on his pony with his wife or lass mounted behind him'.

On a rounded promontory to the north of Traigh Eais lies Dun Scurrival. Little is left of what is thought to have been a galleried dun—a circular prehistoric fortress with galleries in its walls.

There is the stump of a small but massive square tower on an islet in Loch Tangusdale, and there are also a few chambered cairns and a number of standing stones. The antiquities of Barra, apart from Kiessimul Castle, are otherwise of minor interest.

Kiessimul Castle

The castle is perched on a rock in the centre of Castle Bay, and covers it completely. The latter is made of black flinty crush-rock which is extremely hard, so it has been able to withstand the attacks of weather and the battering of the sea. The earliest structure is thought to have been a great curtain or ring wall, adjusted to the contours of the rock base. Midway on the eastern front was the only entrance, defended by a portcullis. Later a square keep tower, or donjon, was erected on

H

the south-eastern side, the original entrance being blocked up and a new portal being made close to the keep so that it could be kept under surveillance at all times. Within the courtyard are a hall, chapel and other buildings now restored by the late MacNeil of Barra. Both the curtain wall and the tower retain the early medieval arrangements for crowning the wall-heads with wooden galleries designed for defence.

The castle was built from local stone and mortar, most likely by Hebridean masons under the direction of a master mason who seemed to be well abreast of contemporary military practice. A conspicuous feature of the masonry is bands of large stone up-ended or set on edge, with the broad flat surfaces to the exterior. This technique is common in early medieval structures in the Hebrides, probably to reduce the penetration of rain and seawater.

In 1939 the old castle gate of Kiessimul was found doing duty as the base for a peat stack in Sponish, North Uist, and was offered by the trustees of Sir Arthur Campbell-Orde, the proprietor of North Uist, to the MacNeil of Barra, to be erected on the restored castle. How the door came to be in North Uist is a very long story, beginning when the then MacNeil left Kiessimul early in the eighteenth century, taking this two-leaved gate with him, for Eoligarry, on Barra. When his effects at Eoligarry were disposed of later, the gate was bought by a doctor in North Uist. Its subsequent whereabouts are unknown, until it was found under the peat stack.

In 1937 Robert Lister MacNeil, Chief of the Clan MacNeil, bought Kiessimul Castle and some 12,000 acres of Barra to become a landed proprietor in the country of his ancestors. As a professional architect, he took a great interest in the restoration of the castle, beginning work on it in 1938. When he had finished, the castle had become both a family home and a shrine for the clan. In 1959 the MacNeil moved into a small two-storey building within the castle walls. He died in 1970 and is at rest in the vault in the castle chapel.

RECORDED HISTORY

The history of Barra before the upheavals of the last century is not without interest. Barra is mentioned in eleventh-century documents, before which date the Hebrides were under Norse supremacy. Norse literature contains many references to the Hebrides. Of particular interest is the record of the number of visits paid to the islands by kings, including Cearball of Ossory (in Ireland); Harald; Rollo, who founded Normandy; Eric, who succeeded Harald on his abdication in AD 930; Olaf; Magnus Barefoot; and Olav Bitling. A daughter of Olav married Somerled of Argyll, who founded the ruling dynasty known for generations as the Lords of the Isles, from whom the MacNeils obtained the overlordship of Barra. The MacNeils held Barra from at least 1427, when Gill-Amhanain MacNeil received the title by charter from Alexander, Lord of the Isles, in favour of whom the Norsemen had resigned their supremacy in the Hebrides. After the dissolution of the Lordship of the Isles, the MacNeil charter was confirmed by King James IV in 1495. It is likely, however, that the family was closely associated with Barra long before the island and its satellites were given into its charge.

The MacNeils played many roles in the history of the Highlands and of Scotland, and were usually found at the centre, or very close to it, of not a few disturbances. Roderick (Ruairidh 's Tartair—Rory the Turbulent) MacNeil, Chief of the Clan during the reign of King James VI, seized an English vessel off the shores of Ireland, and there was an immediate complaint by Queen Elizabeth I to the King of Scots, accusing him of piracy. MacNeil was summoned to appear before the Privy Council in Edinburgh to answer for his conduct. He ignored the command and a ship was sent to fetch him from Barra. He was tricked on board and carried off to Edinburgh to face the charges. When asked why he had attacked a ship of a friendly nation, he told King James that he had imagined that he (MacNeil) had done the king a service by injuring 'the woman who had murdered His Majesty's mother'. This reply saved MacNeil from the gallows, and he was punished instead by the forfeiture of his estate. It was restored to him soon afterwards, under the guarantee of MacKenzie of Kintail, on payment of an annual rent of £20 Scots plus a hawk when required. The superiority of Barra later passed from Kintail to the MacDonalds of Sleat, with whom it still nominally remains.

The Barra islanders, being Catholic and adventurous (they fought under Claverhouse at the Battle of Killicrankie and were 'out' in the 1715 Rising), might have been expected to be in the forefront of Prince Charles Edward's supporters. They were not, however, for understandable reasons. The island, because of its known religious and political sympathies, knew of the prince's landing on Eriskay, and the anchoring of the ship *Du Teillay*, piloted by MacNeil's piper, in Barra Sound. But MacNeil was not on the island at that time, and there was no real idea among the islanders of what the prince intended to do when his ship left for Loch nan Uamh on the mainland of Scotland. There was news also of the refusal of MacDonald of Boisdale, South Uist, to help the prince. These reasons, together with the urgent need to secure as much as possible of the crops in the second of two wet summers, resulted in the islanders remaining on Barra. And when news of the progress of the rising eventually reached Barra, the point of no return at Derby had most likely come and gone, and the Barra men felt they could play no special role then in the Jacobite cause.

There is, however, documentary evidence that MacNeil supported the venture from the sidelines. In November 1745 a Spanish ship, commanded by Don Ultan Kindelan of the Untonia Regiment of Spanish Infantry, landed 2,500 stands of arms with £4,000 on Barra, to be later distributed to the mainland forces by an officer of the same regiment, Don Mauricio McMahon. This man was later captured and the many documents he carried fell into the hands of Hanoverian agents, implicating many islands chiefs. Among the documents were two signed by MacNeil: 'I the Lord of Barra will account for ten Pounds Sterling Recd from Lieut MacMahon for Suply to bring up my men for his Rl Hs Service', and 'I the Lord of Barra do promise Lieut MacMahon to be out with my men to convey Pastich of War for his Rl Hs use & will Account for what cost he might be at by my delaying of him or frachting boats for bringing my men to main land.'

This evidence of support for the prince resulted in MacNeil's arrest and imprisonment, first at Inverness and later on board the infamous rat-ship *Pamela*, anchored in Tilbury. It is said that he turned King's Evidence, though there is no firm evidence. In any case, all MacNeil's connections with the rising were well known to Government agents and he had probably realised the futility of denial. He was never prosecuted. Andrew Lang, in his book *Pickle the Spy*, mentions that in 1750 Lochgarry reported to the prince in exile that MacNeil of Barra would bring 150 men to aid a new rising in the Highlands. This scheme was betrayed by Pickle. In 1758 MacNeil's son and heir sailed to Canada, where he died in Quebec, leaving his son to be brought up as a Protestant by a Protestant.

The last MacNeil owner of Barra was Roderick, who entered the army and rose through the ranks to become a lieutenant-general. Barra was sold by Roderick's creditors in 1838. General MacNeil died in London in 1863, the last MacNeil of Barra. He was succeeded in the chieftainship by Lachlan MacNeil of Brevaig Farm, Vernon River, Prince Edward Island, from whom is descended the present chief—the twenty-sixth, and the forty-sixth from Niall of the Nine Hostages, King of Ireland.

NINETEENTH CENTURY

As in many other parts of the Highlands and Islands, the old social order crumbled during the nineteenth century. During the intercensal period 1841–51 the population fell by 20 per cent to a figure lower than its level 50 years previously. It was during this period that Colonel Gordon offered to sell the island to the Government as a penal colony; the offer was refused. After 1851, despite the fall in population, there still remained the problem of land shortage on Barra, which led to a prolonged period of agrarian discontent. The problem, common to the Hebrides, produced riots throughout the islands, in consequence of which Government warships were sent to patrol the Minch waters. A further manifestation of the Government's alarm at the agitated state of the Highlands, which had taken on a political flavour when crofter representatives were elected to Parliament, was the Napier Commission, set up by the second Gladstone Government 'to inquire into the condition of the Crofters and Cottars in the Highlands and Islands of Scotland, and all matters affecting the same, or relating thereto'.

The root of the trouble lay in (1) the lack of security of tenure, which in effect gave estate managements complete power over the lives of their small tenants, and (2) with the fundamentally unstable economic situation whereby large farms, often the creations of earlier clearances, marched with overcrowded crofting townships where the tenants were always short of suitable land. The Napier Commission visited Barra and took evidence on 26 May 1883. The first and principal witness to give evidence was Michael Buchanan, a crofter-fisherman from Borve, who, with others, had been elected by the crofters of Borve to speak for them. Those elected to give evidence were not wholly beholding to the landowner, and so could speak more freely.

The outcome of the Napier Commission was the Crofters' Holdings (Scotland) Act of 1886, which granted security of tenure (subject to the fulfilment of certain statutory conditions), compensation for improvements carried out by the tenants, facilities for the enlargement of holdings, and the fixing of fair rents. This last requirement was carried out by a body of three commissioners, one of whom was to be a Gaelic speaker, the only time in British history when a knowledge of Gaelic has been statutorily required of a person holding a public appointment in the Highlands and Islands, where the Gaelic-speaking population at that time numbered well over 300,000. Later this body of commissioners became known as the Scottish Land Court.

Despite the dawning of a new day for the Barra crofters, land long remained in short supply. In 1901 the Congested Districts Board bought 3,000 acres of the Eoligarry Farm to create fifty-eight new holdings (see p 140). The breaking up of Vatersay Farm is described elsewhere in this book (see p 169). After World War I the remainder of Eoligarry Farm was raided successfully. There are now no large farms on Barra.

POPULATION

The first reasonably accurate figure given for the population of Barra is 1,285 in the year 1750. However, Webster's Return for the same year shows 1,150. Whether there was a decrease, or whether the original figure was a rough estimate, out by as much as 135 persons, is not clear. From 1771, however, there was a distinct rise in population until the period 1821–31, when a slight decrease occurred. From 1841 the figures are subject to the influence of the clearances. After 1861 there was a steady rise in the population until the census of 1911 recorded the highest figure—2,620. The prosperity of the fishing industry accounted for this maximum, which then began to fall away as that industry declined. It was still possible before World War II to live in the Hebrides on a modest income, and many islanders probably preferred that to becoming expatriates in cities like Glasgow. This preference would account for the decrease in population between 1921 and 1947 of only about 400 persons. By the time of the 1961 census, however, the decline became more rapid, and the estimated figure issued in

1971 by the Registrar-General for Scotland was only 1,159 persons.

The Barra population figures (round figures to the nearest hundred) are shown in Table 4.

TABLE 4   *Population of Barra*

Date	Population	Date	Population	Date	Population
1750	1,285	1831	2,100	1931	2,300
	(Church records)	1841	2,400	1947	2,112
1750	1,150	1851	1,900		(West Highland
	(Webster's Return)	1861	1,900		Survey)
1771	1,395	1871	2,000	1961	1,600
	(Walker's Return)	1881	2,200	1966	1,467
1791	1,604	1891	2,400		(sample census)
	(*OS Account*)	1901	2,500	1969	1,152
1801	1,900	1911	2,620		(estimate)
1811	2,100	1921	2,500	1971	1,159
1821	2,300				

ISLAND CLEARANCES

A partial clearance took place in 1851 ,the year in which the Secretary of the Royal Patriotic Society stated that there were some 50,000 people in the Western Highlands and Islands of Scotland who were very nearly destitute, if not entirely so. Though this was probably an exaggerated estimate, it was a fact that distress was acute in many Highland districts. As if to underline their distress, in February 1851 sixty-one destitute people made their way from Barra to Inverness and sat down in front of the Town House to see what the authorities would do for them. About forty of them were sent to the parish poorhouse, while the remainder were accommodated in lodgings. After a few days this group drifted eastwards, hoping to find employment in the fisheries on the Buchan coast. Later, faced with fresh arrivals, the Inverness Inspector of the Poor tried to recover the cost of their sustenance from the Barra Parochial Board. But the latter pointed out that they were not responsible for the able-bodied, and further demanded that any of their charges under the care of the Inspector be sent back to Barra immediately. Eventually these wanderers from Barra found work near Inverness, where they lived in great poverty.

As was the case elsewhere throughout the Highlands and Islands, the clearances were effected with great cruelty. The agents of the Barra and South Uist proprietor, Colonel Gordon, forced people on to waiting ships, which were chartered to remove people from his estates. Eventually many Barra people found themselves in Canada. The *Quebec Times* had this to say in 1851:

> We noticed in our last the deplorable condition of the 600 paupers who were sent to this country from the Kilrush Unions. We have today a still more dismal picture to draw. Many of our readers may not be aware that there lives such a personage as Colonel Gordon, proprietor of large estates, South Uist and Barra, in the Highlands of Scotland. We are sorry to be obliged to introduce him to their notice under circumstances which will not give them a very favourable opinion of his character and heart.
>
> It appears that tenants of the above-mentioned estates were on the verge of starvation, and had probably become an eyesore to the gallant Colonel. He decided on shipping them to America.

RELIGIOUS HISTORY

For at least sixteen centuries Barra has been an island devoted to the Catholic faith, first that derived from the early Columban tradition and the teachings of the Celtic Church, and later the Roman concepts which exist today. Christianity was introduced throughout the Hebrides during the sixth and seventh centuries AD, though preliminary work may have begun as early as the fifth century, for in or about 447 the See of the Isles was founded by St Patrick, and Germanus was created its first bishop. Until the end of the fourteenth century it was united to the See of Sodor, but it fell vacant for more than 300 years after the Reformation, from the death of Roderick MacLean in 1553. Since 1878 the combined Sees of Argyll and the Isles have administered the area, which includes the other Catholic island of South Uist, and small Catholic communities such as that in Stornoway, Lewis.

In 1651 Clanranald appealed from South Uist to the Congregation of Propaganda in Rome for priests. Eventually St Vincent de Paul, the founder of the Lazarists, provided missionary help in the form of three priests, of whom Fr Duggan was responsible for the Inner and Outer Hebrides. He worked for a solid 5 year period, by the end of which time the folk from Benbecula to Barra Head had been largely reconciled to the faith. In Barra Fr Duggan is commemorated by a pass over the hills— Bealach a' Dhugain.

By 1671 Barra and the Hebridean Mission generally had been placed under the care of Blessed Oliver Plunket, the martyred Archbishop of Armagh in Northern Ireland. Though beset with the troubles in Ireland arising from the Cromwellian devastation of that land, the Primate contemplated a visit to the Hebrides: '. . . it will be necessary for me to bring a priest and a servant with me and to dress after the manner of these people which is very different from that of every part of the globe.'

While the islands generally escaped the worst effects of seventeenth-century religious bigotry, persecution of Catholics by Episcopalians and Presbyterians being particularly intense on the Scottish mainland, it was not until Clanranald in South Uist and MacNeil in Barra apostatised that the real persecution began. While the term of Clanranald's apostasy was very bad in Uist, MacNeil was the lesser tyrant in the cause of Protestantism. Nevertheless, Protestant tenants were sent from North Uist to be planted in Barra from time to time, and given the best holdings. The Barra folk held close to their faith, however, despite the fact that their chief's son had been left by his father to be brought up by a Protestant relative.

The year 1829 saw the Roman Catholic Relief Act, and since then the succession of priests has continued uneventfully to minister to a Catholic flock which is as faithful today to its religion as it has strived to be for many centuries. The church at Castlebay, completed in 1889, is a feature of the town, lying as it does on a spendid rise to dominate the whole scene. It is named 'Our Lady, Star of the Sea'. The 'mother' church of Barra is at Craigstone, built on the site of an earlier church, and there is a third church at Northbay, built in 1906.

Notwithstanding the fact that Barra has always been Catholic, other denominations have had a foothold on the island. The first established minister (Church of Scotland) on Barra was the Rev John MacPherson (1734). The general tendency of these ministers was to serve the establishment on the island and to subscribe to the repressive measures which the chiefs and landlords took to impose on their tenants. The conduct of the Rev Henry Beatson (1847–71) was particularly notable for the officious servility he paid to the landlord at the time and for the active part he played in aiding forced evictions and emigrations from the island.

CROFTING

The economy of the Barra community has always been based on the land, which provided a subsistence, with the help of coastal fishing. Only during the last century or so has maritime fishing been a significant activity. Before that, the sea was a high road to plunder, the MacNeils striking out from the island as mercenaries and pirates. Manuscripts record that in 1589 600 Barra men and their kinsmen raided Erris in Co Mayo, Ireland, and another body foraged in Ulster. They 'killed six hundred cows, freighting their galleys with the spoil, and five hundred cows, besides, they carried to an island, and there killed them and took away their hides and tallow.' No doubt these by-products found their way to a ready and profitable market. These were predatory raids intended to fill empty larders and pockets and had little or no political significance.

Writing in 1549, Dean Monro stated that Barra was fruitful in corn, codfish, ling and that other white fish abounded in the seas. He mentioned also that the cockle bed to the north of the island was an important source of food for the poorer folk. In 1620 Walter MacFarlane wrote that an 'abundance of fish is slaine in the sea of Barray . . . And there is abundance of choice little cockle shells found.'

As part of his contribution to the *Old Statistical Account of Scotland*, the Rev Edward MacQueen wrote:

> Agriculture has been almost invariably the same here (as in most of the western isles) for time immemorial, till within these last five years, when Mr Macneil, the proprietor, returned from visiting foreign counties, has begun to introduce the method used in the low country, as far as he thinks the soil and climate can admit of . . . there are some meadows that yield three successive crops with one coat of manure, viz., one of potatoes and two of oats. The people here use the plough for the most part; but in their rocky ground they dig or turn up the ground with a kind of lever, which they call the crooked spade . . . The principal crop here is barley and potatoes [the potato was introduced into Barra in 1752]; there is some small black oats and a little rye.

Writing in 1840, as part of his contribution to the *New Statistical Account for Scotland*, the Rev Alexander Nicholson, Church of Scotland minister on Barra, states:

> . . . the black cattle of Barray are very good. The stock reared by the proprietor himself was considered as one of the best in the Highlands. The small horses reared by the crofters are much esteemed, both for their symmetry and hardiness; of these they keep too many, to the detriment of their black cattle, at the same time they find them exceedingly useful for the manufacture of their kelp, and for leading seaweed from their shores for manure, though a much fewer number might serve them for every useful purpose. No regular sheepstock has been introduced into this parish until last year . . . every crofter has his own small plough and a couple of ponies with which he turns up his ground . . .

All the agricultural land on Barra is now held as crofters' smallholdings. Methods of cultivation depend on land relief and soil conditions, the spade being used in those areas to which a tractor cannot gain access.

The Barra pony was once a very popular animal, bred on the island, but the demand has declined steadily in recent years. The stock is small and hardy, and high prices were once obtained for these beasts.

An association of Barra crofters uses the southern islands of Sandray, Pabbay, Mingulay and Berneray as grazing land. The stock is of a high quality. The crofts are small, usually under 10 acres on average, with grazing rights on the hills feued from the MacNeil of Barra, who owns half the island, and from the Department of Agriculture, which owns the other half. Rents vary from about £2 to £8 per annum. There are a large number of vacant croft houses in the island, and it has been suggested that these might be let to summer visitors. Many crofts in Barra are sublet, as a result of the 1961 Act, which enables a crofter to sublet his croft with the consent of the Crofters Commission.

The number of crofts on Barra (380) has remained constant in recent years, indicating perhaps that they provide a good basic income for their owners, whether or not this is supplemented by income from other sources. Arable crops are grown mainly for feeding to stock, the crofters' cash income being derived from the sale of livestock, store cattle in particular. The sandy soils of Barra provide good grazing land, and in a number of parts of the island stock can be wintered with little or no hand feeding. Each croft is more or less self-supporting in dairy produce, though the emphasis is on the raising of stores; hardy beef breeds and crosses are best suited to the conditions on the island. Highland and Highland-Shorthorn crosses are considered the most hardy types. Shorthorn-Aberdeen Angus crosses are also common, although many cattle are of mixed descent. Young stock are sold in May as one-, two- or three-year olds; and older cattle are sold for slaughtering or breeding during the autumn sales. There are about 2,000 cattle, dairy and beef, on the island.

The sheep on Barra are mostly of the Scottish blackfaced breed. In most townships sheep stocks are individually owned by the crofters. There are about 13,000 sheep on the island, and their clip generally makes its way to Lewis for the Harris Tweed industry.

Poultry are kept on all crofts, mainly for domestic use. Pigs, as in other parts of the Highlands, are unpopular in Barra, possibly reflecting a very long-standing dislike of the pig by the Celt.

In 1901 the Congested Districts Board bought 3,000 acres of the farm at Eoligarry and created fifty-eight new holdings, on which crofters from other parts of the island were settled. It was at first intended to settle these as owner-occupiers, but after a short time the occupiers became tenants of the Board at their own request. Soon after World War I the remainder of Eoligarry Farm was raided and settled on by crofters. The Eoligarry settlement, with that on Vatersay, is reckoned to be a model of its kind, with applied standards of management that have not been without influence elsewhere in the Highlands and Islands.

FISHING

Although commercial fishing was begun in the waters of the Minch during the sixteenth century by Dutch, French and Spanish fishermen, little interest was shown in it by the men of Barra, except as an inshore activity to supplement their diet. Martin Martin, who visited Barra about 1695 says: 'There is plenty of cod and ling to be got on the east and south sides of this island. Several ships from Orkney come hither in summer, and afterwards return laden with cod and ling.' Also according to Martin, the herring net was in use in Barra at this time, though there is no mention of herring fishing; but it can be assumed that as these nets were used for catching large quantities of salmon, herring shoals which came in close to land would also not be ignored.

The fishing industry expanded slowly until the end of the eighteenth century, at which stage MacNeil of Barra proposed that the local fishermen should cast losts for the fishing banks round the island's coastline. This scheme proved to be most successful, and had the added advantage in that it eliminated any possible disputes. It was further improved on when the Barra waters were demarcated and charted by the Marine Survey Service of the Royal Navy, and the fishing grounds were located by means of landmarks on the adjacent hills and headlands on the island.

The grounds for great-line fishing were located a few miles from the eastern coastline, as well as around Barra Head. Ling, cod, skate and halibut were the predominant species, though cod and ling were favoured because they were easy to cure and to dry. Great-line fishing was also carried out on the west side of Barra, but only when conditions were favourable. Although there were a few families on the island who could build boats, most of the craft used were built on the littoral of the Moray Firth or Aberdeenshire and were lugger-rigged. The boats were sturdy and seaworthy, with a keel length in the region of 30ft. The lines were deposited in the banks during the daytime and left overnight. On the following day the boats went to their respective lines, marked by buoys, and either hauled in, re-baited and cast, or else hauled in and cast a fresh-baited set of lines.

The catch was bought by the shore-based curing stations, each boat contracting to supply fish to a particular station. The fish were sold not by weight but by capitation, latterly about 7½d for ling and 6d for cod. The fish were put into brine overnight if the catch was heavy, otherwise they were fresh-gutted, headed, split and boned by the gutting-women. The pickling process was continued after a further period and the fish were then exposed to wind and sun to dry. They were exported in bundles of stated numbers and shipped to the Clyde ports to be sold either to Scottish fish merchants or made ready for re-export, particularly to Catholic countries such as Spain.

Small-line fishing was carried out on the inshore sandbanks in the straits between Barra's satellite islands. The bulk of the fish caught in this way was used domestically. Shellfish were also caught, lobsters in the early days being sold to local merchants at a standard price and subsequently sold by weight at a general market, such as at Billingsgate, London. Cockles, once a staple food in Barra, particularly when the crops failed, were gathered from the Traigh Mhor.

In 1869 James Methuen, one of the leading herring-curers in Scotland, decided to use Castlebay as a herring port. Within a few years it had become a serious rival to other Hebridean ports such as Lochboisdale and Stornoway. It is on record that there were occasions when Castlebay's spacious natural harbour could not hold all the boats which required berths. Some boats had to land their catch at Northbay and on the adjacent island of Vatersay. Much of the catch was made by boats from the east and north-east ports of Scotland. Little contribution to the total catch was made by Barra men, mainly because their boats were too small to venture far from the shore. Barra fishermen, however, were more venturesome than most, as they went farther out to sea with their great-lines. But, like most other Hebridean fishermen, they found themselves continually in debt to the curers who supplied them with their boats and gear. Most Barra men lacked the necessary capital to buy the larger boats necessary for successful herring fishing in the Minch.

There is no doubt, however, that the herring industry, with Castlebay as one of its main centres, brought prosperity to Barra. About 1886 up to 400 boats (averaging from 15 to 20 tons burden) congregated in the bay from the beginning of May

Page 143
Harvesting on
Eriskay

Page 144
Creagorry,
Benbecula, and the
waters of the South
Ford

to the end of June each year. During the height of the season some 2,000 persons were employed on the island by the small regiment of fish-curers, who ran up temporary huts and bothies surrounded by piles of barrels destined for St Petersburg, Konigsburg, Danzig, Hamburg and Stettin. Daily catches amounted to many thousands of cran (the cran was the standard measure and consisted of four baskets, each having a capacity of about 1,000 herrings of average size).

Barra men were mostly employed on boats, which arrived in Castlebay with only skeleton crews. The men received a retaining fee of about £5 and 5 per cent of the net earnings. A pound of strong black twist tobacco was included in their emoluments. The Barra women were also engaged in the industry as gutters and salters, working in teams of three. Two did the gutting while the third packed and salted the herrings in the barrels. Packing was a skilled job and an expert could handle up to 100,000 herrings in a single day's work.

For a number of decades before and after the turn of this century between 600 and 1,000 Barra women were employed regularly at herring gutting and kindred occupations, their net earnings for a season of 29 weeks being about £14. But slowly the industry declined, particularly after World War I, when Castlebay was dependent for its prosperity entirely on the export of cured herring. The quality of the fish was very high, however, and Castlebay herring continued to fetch top prices in German and Russian markets. Then catches began to vary in quality and quantity from year to year. In 1931, which was a good year, as many as 200 boats were using the port, but other years saw only a shadow of the former glory. Some of the decline was due to the large numbers of men who had left their homes to fight in World War I. When they returned, there was not the same number of boats to absorb them. After 1931 the industry declined sharply to receive a final blow in 1939 with the advent of World War II.

In 1933 the island had ninety-four boats (twenty-three sail, the remainder motor-driven) with a total of 276 tons and employing some 102 men. The total catch for that year was valued at £191,961 (31,479cwt). Shellfish accounted for £1,519. The Barra ports included Castlebay, Bruernish, Ault, Earsary, Breivig and Skallary.

After World War II Castlebay was reopened as a herring port, but the fishing from Barra was not so profitable as that from ports such as Lerwick and Wick, where most of the Scottish herring catch was processed for reduction to meal and oil, a facility which Castlebay did not have. But the Barra men clung to their fishing industry, and their determination has been recognised in recent years by the Highlands and Islands Development Board. There was a significant increase in the value of shellfish catches, the 1948 catch, for instance, being worth £17,572, about ten times as much as in 1938. This also was a pointer to the future.

In the 1950s the Government-sponsored Outer Hebrides Fisheries Training Scheme was introduced to encourage fishing throughout the Hebrides. By 1962 nine boats had been provided under the Scheme for crews from Lewis, Scalpay, Eriskay and Barra (two). Most of the boats were equipped for dual-purpose work—ring-net fishing during the normal herring season and nephrops trawling at other times. Subsequently the Highlands and Islands Development Board extended the scheme by providing more boats and Barra was among the islands to benefit from the £500,000 the Board committed itself to spend on building up a Minch-based fleet. Six vessels now operate from Barra.

Recently, however, a blow to the status of Castlebay as a herring port was administered by the Herring Industry Board, which prohibited the sale of herring from certain Scottish ports, but during the winter of 1970 Castlebay received a welcome boost when a steady stream of klondykers (factory ships) arrived from the Continent and the Faroes to buy Minch-caught herring for shipment to and subsequent processing in foreign ports. This trade was developed because of the scarcity of North Sea herring, and gave Castlebay its busiest winter for many years, with casual work for unemployed men, greatly improved harbour dues and general benefits to the islanders. In one month more than 14,000 crans, valued at £70,000, had been klondyked.

The Sea League

During the 1930s Castlebay was the centre of an organisation concerned with Minch fishing called the Sea League. The main reason behind the formation of the League was the serious illegal trawling which was taking place in Minch waters, and particularly within the statutory 3 mile limit, by English trawlers. In 1895 an Act of Parliament had provided for the formation of fishing districts all round Scotland, if a sufficient proportion of those connected in any way with fishing in an area applied to their various County Councils to move in the matter of forming these districts. The Act also said that a 14 mile limit would be imposed as soon as the North Sea Convention met and approved such a limit (the Convention members included Britain, Denmark, Holland, Belgium, France and Germany). The people who opposed the 14 mile limit were the trawler owners of Hull, Grimsby and Fleetwood, the very people who were fishing illegally, and their actions prevented the Convention from being summoned and the fishing districts formed.

The Sea League was constituted in 1933 '. . . to demand the same protection for the livelihood of the crofting fisherman as is given to the sporting fishing of the landowners themselves', and managed to stimulate the Government into preparing legislation to increase the penalties for illegal trawling. But it met with real opposition from the trawling interests. Indeed, it was not until 1964 that the Fishery Limits Act was passed, long after serious damage had been done to the Minch fishing grounds by illegal trawling and indiscriminate dredging of the sea bottom, which destroyed spawning beds and nearly brought herring fishing to an end.

GENERAL EMPLOYMENT

On Barra, outside agriculture and fishing, very little in the way of manufacturing and service industries has found its way into the island's economy, though in recent years some brave attempts have been made. There are fleeting and tantalising references in past documents to the 'Glassaree', seemingly a factory established by the MacNeil of Barra for making washing soda and iodine and other by-products used in the making of glass. Whether glass was actually made in the factory is not known; it is more likely that the establishment was devoted to the production of glass-making elements and so acquired the common name by which it was known.

In 1967 the Highlands and Islands Development Board announced rather proudly and indeed with some justification that 'Technology comes to Barra'. The occasion was the opening of a new spectacle-frame factory at Northbay, in the former school at a cost of £10,000. The initial intake of employees was twelve, two men and ten girls, with a hope that the workforce would be increased to thirty within a year. The firm's owners were more than pleased at the speed with which the Barra workers mastered fairly complicated operations and with the standard of work produced. There was the possibility that the Barra factory would become established as the main base for short-run mass production. The wages paid were exactly the same as those paid to the firm's employees in their Glasgow factory.

The Development Board expressed the hope that the venture would prove to other firms manufacturing high-value light-weight goods that worthwhile commercial operations could be carried out in the so-called remote west, but in October 1969 it was announced that the firm had gone into liquidation, and with it went the Barra venture, together with an associated plant at Campbeltown, Argyll. In a space of 2 years a venture started full of hope had gone to the wall, but the potential was definitely there. With such melodic names as Morven, Catrina and Torridon, the spectacle frames from Barra had attracted the interests of the American market.

Another venture, on a much smaller scale, which still survives and has found a growing market, is the Barra Perfume Company. The product is made in a tiny factory run by two men at Tangusdale, near Halaman Bay on the south-west of the island. The perfumes are hand-made in small individual batches by half a dozen girls. The low overheads of this firm have resulted in its products being marketed at really competitive prices. The names of the perfumes ring with the sights and sounds of the Hebrides—Tangle, Plaid, Dark Glen, Legend, Caluna, Love Lilt, and so on.

During 1969 another science-based industry, the manufacture of thermostat components and micro-switches, opened an extension factory in Barra. Barra Assemblies Ltd, a subsidiary of Otter Controls Ltd, provided jobs for six people, mostly female. Because the components and assembled parts are small, light and of high value, they are moved in and out of Barra by air.

At Vaslain, behind Traigh Mhor, is a small but interesting industry—the manufacture of shell grit 'Barra Harl', used for harling. The shells in the vicinity have a high lime content and are extremely white, so that the rough-cast which they produce is at once durable and comely. The shell grit is also used in chickenfeed stuffs.

At Allusdale, a small craft activity, Peggy Angus & Associates, produces sea stones decorated with Celtic designs, and hand-painted wallpapers.

These industrial pockets were the result of the combined work of the Barra Council of Social Service and the Development Board. They have proved that, with careful attention to management, small industries can be made to pay.

At the time of writing there are hopes that a shellfish-processing plant will be established on Barra. The islanders see such a plant fitting into the island's traditional pattern of life, and there is a ready market for crabs, of which there is an abundance around the Barra shores. A development which would spring from this new activity would be an increase in the number of Barra lobster boats, which at present number eight or so.

One source of revenue for the Barra community is young Barra seamen. As many as 60 per cent (about 400) of Barra's menfolk are estimated to be serving in the Merchant service because of the lack of suitable work and opportunities at home. A rough estimate has revealed that each man sends between £30 and £40 per month home to his family, which income constitutes a significant element in the Barra economy.

The tourist industry has been slow to develop, although there has always been a traditional service industry catering for visitors. The original inn at Northbay was known as Tiorbagh Inn. In the reign of King Charles I a law decreed that inns separated by straits were to be built opposite each other. Pollachar Inn (at the southern end of South Uist) paired an inn called Keil Inn. Later, it was thought that a more convenient site would be at Tiorbagh and the structure was completed in the 1820s. The inn was very small at first and towards the end of the century was extended and heightened. There was a taproom at one end and coachhouses at the other, and a well stocked vegetable garden was established.

Tiorbagh was always very busy. The expanding herring industry brought fishermen and fish-curers from the east coast of Scotland. Nearby the herring was poured on to the ground on the Ardveanish side of the bay and women knelt on the grass to do the gutting. The stone 'stations' they used can still be traced. Markets were also held at nearby Loch-an-Duin twice yearly, in June and September. These were important occasions. Drovers came from the mainland and adjacent isles to buy cattle and horses. Barra ponies in particular were in great demand. To supplement the provisions of Tiorbagh Inn, innkeepers from Uist and Skye came to set up their marquees for the sale of whisky. Merchants came from the mainland to set up tents to sell their merchandise. About the turn of this century the inn was closed. It seems that too much drinking went on there and poor families tended to suffer; eventually pressure was brought to bear on the tenant and he left the district. Later the building was let out in tenements to several families and part of it was taken over by the Local Nursing Association as quarters for the first qualified nurse appointed to the district in 1921.

In March 1970 it was announced by the Highlands and Islands Development Board that an hotel was to be built at Tangusdale, on Barra, the second in a chain of such hotels designed to expand the tourist trade for specific areas in the Western Highlands. Research carried out by the Board's tourist division, and advice from tourist consultants, suggested that Barra had a great tourist potential and that, to exploit it, and to ensure a reasonable financial return on capital, the hotel should be of reasonable size (40 bedrooms) and should operate all the year round. It opened in 1974.

ROADS

Barra is served by a single-track ring-road, some 14 miles long, which was completed in 1930 and connects the main townships. Though the road provisions were extremely primitive and rather unsuitable for vehicles, the first motor car made its appearance on Barra in 1926, to be the forerunner of many others. In time, however, exasperated by the state of the roads while being under the legal obligation to pay the road tax, an increasing number of car owners rebelled against payment. The subsequent affair became a boon for headline writers in the national dailies.

In 1884 a telegraph cable was extended from Lochboisdale on South Uist to Castlebay, thus greatly improving communications between the mainland and Barra, which had until then depended on the mail connections via Dunvegan (Skye) and Lochmaddy, through Benbecula, South Uist, and the ferry across the Barra Sound. In 1938 the General Post Office acquired a site for a small telephone exchange and in September 1939 Castlebay was first recorded in the 'List of Exchanges' for that year. There are at present almost 200 ordinary subscribers on the island, and fourteen call offices. A radio link exists between Barra, via Tobermoray (Mull), and Oban. There are five post offices, at Borve, Castlebay, Eoligarry, Northbay and Skallary. First-class mail arrives with the Glasgow plane thrice weekly in winter and daily during the summer months. Second-class mail and parcels are carried by steamer thrice weekly. The island is well served with roadside letterboxes, which are emptied daily.

FOLKLORE

For almost a century now Barra has been recognised as an important depository of Gaelic traditions. Though a great deal has been collected, there still remains much interesting field-work for the folklorist, musicologist and anthropologist. The rich and varied Gaelic tradition was preserved by persons such as the late John MacPherson (The Coddy) of Northbay. Oral tradition, which scorned the printed word for its continued survival, was served particularly well. Many continuous folktales recorded in recent years have lasted days!

About 85 per cent of the Barra population are bilingual in Gaelic and English, and the 1961 census showed that only thirty-eight people conversed in Gaelic only. The culture derived from the language has been faithfully preserved by the islanders. Three collectors—Alexander Carmichael (*Carmina Gadelica*), J. F. Campbell (*Popular Tales of the West Highlands*), and Mrs Kennedy Fraser (*Songs of the Hebrides*)—have been greatly indebted to Barra singers and reciters for their literary and musical material. Barra has produced many literary efforts which contain the essence of what might be termed 'folk literature'—material derived from within the island's community and produced for its own consumption. An example of this is seen in Colm O Lochlainn's *Deoch-slainte nan Gillean*.

ISLAND LIFE

As with most island communities, communications, high freight charges for materials imported from the mainland, lack of opportunities for work among both unemployed males and school-leavers, and lack of advanced schooling facilities, have created problems. Proposals for general Highland development, as projected by the Highlands and Islands Development Board, have produced both joy and uncertainty. A suggestion, made in 1970, that Mallaig rather than Oban become the mainland terminal for the Outer Hebrides brought the quick response from Barra that such a move would increase fares and food prices by 7 per cent. This could only accelerate the present rate of emigration from the island. In 1968 it was shown in *The Scotsman*'s Prices Index that the cost of a week's groceries bought in Barra was at least 10 per cent above their cost in other marginally less remote parts on the Scottish mainland. An island merchant bought 2 tons of potatoes from the mainland, to find that the bill for carriage was almost the same as the cost of the potatoes. The high prices for basic commodities are the result of local shops being unable to buy as competitively as city retailers, not having access to daily competitive supplies. Shipping and delivery charges are often extra on the buyer's account.

Incessant calls have been made for better pier, jetty and

harbour facilities. Castlebay is Barra's main port and the only one where a steamer and freight-carrying vessel can tie up; but the pier is in disrepair, needing £80,000 to be spent on it to bring it up to date with a badly needed extension. The landing jetty at Eoligarry also needs repair, and that would cost some £30,000.

In 1966 the islanders formed the Barra Development Association, which threw up much enthusiasm and many ideas. But it failed to carry out any of the projects the organisers had in mind, despite their strenuous efforts, and ended up without support or funds. As an example of the kind of initiative which existed inside the community one can instance the *Barra Bulletin*, a fortnightly duplicated newspaper, but it lasted only for a few issues.

More recently the Barra and Vatersay Council of Social Service was formed. With about 100 unemployed in Barra, the Council has determined to improve conditions on the island. It approached a Norwegian fish-processing company which had shown an interest in setting up a substantial plant in Castlebay. The company wanted to know first what Barra had to offer in the way of labour, and the Council had to discover the whereabouts of Barra exiles, and get in touch with them to see how many of them would return to the island if a major industry materialised. The results were more than encouraging, the figures revealing that Barra's population could be increased within a year by something like 25 per cent by returning exiles. More than twenty-five applications were received by the local District Council for houses from people living on the Scottish mainland, mostly in Glasgow. The County Council are also looking into a suggestion that instead of building new houses, many of the houses at present lying empty could be renovated. As these houses are scattered throughout the island, an additional advantage would be the avoidance of heavy concentrations of people in one area, as would occur in a typical local authority housing scheme.

The renovation of the shells of almost derelict buildings is at present being carried out by an English-based firm operating a cottage-holidays scheme, in an effort to attract tourists.

With the ever-increasing tendency to centralisation, it will remain to be seen just how long Barra and its folk can remain a distinct community. The effect of such plans as the restructuring of local government in Scotland and Britain's entry into the Common Market are impossible to guess at. One can be certain, however, that the islanders will fight for their own way of life.

6   ERISKAY

IT was perhaps through the Gaelic song-collecting of Marjory Kennedy Fraser that the small island of Eriskay first became known to the world at large. One song in particular, the 'Eriskay Love Lilt', though she had subjected it to a process of emasculation from its original strong Gaelic-based character, was an excellent ambassador for the island and for the Hebrides in general.

The island (Gaelic: Eirisgeigh—Eric's Isle; ON: Eirikr) lies just off the south-eastern tip of South Uist, being separated from the larger island by the Sound of Eriskay. For the visitor weaned on the island's famous song it presents a rather disappointing appearance—unless it is viewed from Ludac on South Uist on a fine summer's day of the kind that casts a blue sea-haze over all the islands. Otherwise, Eriskay is an undistinguished lump of storm-weathered Archean gneiss just under 3 miles in length (N–S) and about 2 miles across at its widest. Its coasts are edged by rocky cliffs except for the sands in the north-west corner. The two main heights are Ben Scrien (609ft) in the north and Ben Stack (403ft) in the south, a geological continuation southwards of the hilly eastern belt of South Uist.

The sea indents the island's eastern side deeply at Acairseid Mhor (Big Harbour). On the western side lies Coilleag a' Phrionnsa (The Prince's Strand), a long stretch of silver sand on which Prince Charles Edward Stewart and his entourage landed on 23 July 1745, his first step on Scottish soil. They could not find any meal or bread to eat, but 'they catched some flounders, which they roasted upon the bare coals in a mean, low hut they had gone into near the shore, and Duncan Cameron stood cook.' On a summer's day the brilliance of the reflected light from the shallow waters and the silver sand of this beach impart an almost magical atmosphere, and one can both understand and sympathise with those who fell under the spell of the Celtic Twilight which was so much in vogue at the turn of this century.

The machair of Eriskay is lush, with pastures of ankle-deep grass stretching to the lower slopes of the island's hills. Farther inland, the hill slopes bear sparse vegetation, exposing smooth ice-rounded grey gneiss to the island sky. Much of the plant life is interesting, nevertheless—marsh marigolds, waterlilies, roseroot, celandine and primrose.

The Eriskay pony is a native in decline, probably fewer than thirty of the species remaining, including two stallions. As a class, it is of great antiquity, the nearest to the native race that peopled Scotland before the arrival of man. It is a docile animal, from 12 to 13 hands high. The foals are born black and grow up white or grey. They have small ears. It is hoped that a new interest in the breed will save it, and that it may once more appear in the mainland market for ponies.

The main settlement on Eriskay is at Haun, which is in ferry-boat contact with Ludac on South Uist, a distance of about 1¾ miles. Haun is joined to Rosinish by a rough path. These two townships are in the north of the island. Another path makes its way southward to provide a link with the crofts at Na Pairceanan by Acairseid Mhor. The seventy crofts on Eriskay are all small, and their owners make more from fishing for herring, lobsters and prawns.

Eriskay supports a shop, a post office, a school and a small church. The island was not always so heavily populated as it has been for the last century, for it had only eight inhabitants in 1764. By 1841 that had risen to eighty. During the following decade a large number of people were evicted from the neighbouring island of Hellisay, and these migrants formed the bulk of the population figures returned for 1851—405. Others came to Eriskay from various parts of the Western Isles. Since then the population fluctuation has been as follows: 1861, 396; 1871, 429; 1881, 466; 1891, 454; 1901, 478; 1931, 420; 1951, 330; 1961, 250; and 1972, 206.

The islanders of Eriskay have always had to rely on fishing for their living, crofting being an incidental occupation. A report of the Crofters Commission noted in 1903:

Eriskay is inhabited by a fishing community. Formerly most of the able-bodied men were in use to go to the East Coast [of Scotland] fishing, but they have not been going in large numbers in recent years. The explanation is that the East Coast fishing has often proved uncertain, and that with the better class of boats now owned by the people they do fully better at home, that is by fishing in the neighbourhood of the island and also in the West Highland lochs, such as Loch-Hourn, Loch-Nevis, and the lochs of Skye.

The yearly routine of Eriskay life may be stated thus: In the early spring the men prosecute the line fishing at home, this work being carried on, whenever the weather permits, from January to the middle of March. The cultivation of the crofts, followed by the casting of the peat supply for the year, is then undertaken. Thereafter they go to the herring fishing in Barra and engage in it from April till the end of June, and sometimes during July. The Barra 'season' usually terminates with the end of June, but if there are herrings on the coast the local crews continue to a later date. After the Barra fishing some young men go as hired hands either to Shetland or to the East coast; but such as have boats and suitable fishing gear remain in home waters—first in the neighbourhood of the island if there be fish, and afterwards in any West Highland loch where herrings are being caught.

In September there is a general ingathering of all the people for the purpose of securing the crops. The winter herring fishing is thereafter prosecuted, either at home or in the West Highland lochs, the Eriskay crews resorting to any place where fair catches are being obtained. If the weather be favourable and the fish plentiful, the herring fishing is continued till Christmas.

Formerly lobster fishing was prosecuted off Eriskay, but in recent years this branch of the fishing industry has been of little or no account. A few of the Eriskay men are sailors and labourers, but fishing and the cultivation of the crofts constitute the main industries of the island. It is difficult to say what an Eriskay man earns as a fisherman throughout the year. To put a cash value on all he gets and consumes at home is practically impossible; but his annual earnings from home are variously estimated at from £40 to nil, according to season and luck. Taking one year with another, the able-bodied man is supposed to bring home about £8 a year in hard cash.

Large numbers of Eriskay women engage in the work of herring gutting at home, in Barra, Shetland, the East coast of Scotland, and the English fishing stations . . . the women who follow this calling not infrequently succeed in bringing home more money than do the men.

The Eriskay cottar, it may be remarked, earns as much money by the fishing as the crofter does, but the want of home produce is a great hardship to him. There is no local market where he can buy milk, for instance, and if he has not a cow feeding on his neighbours' land he has either to beg for milk or do without it. He is in a like position as regards the matter of potato ground.

Gutting was a common summer occupation for the Eriskay women, who went touring the Scottish and English fishing ports to find work. After paying for their expenses the women returned to Eriskay with about £6 each, plus extras in the form of clothing and household goods. Earnings were as high as £8 in a good season. Gutters who were based on Lowestoft only could clear about £14 in a good season.

In 1900 the islanders appealed for a breakwater to secure their fishing boats, for there was then, as today, no proper landing place on the island. The initial scheme proposed was regarded as being too ambitious and a modified scheme was ultimately considered by the Congested Districts Board as being eligible for a grant of £1,500. However, a revised costing revealed the final sum would be in the region of £2,000 and the scheme was allowed to drop, even though the islanders offered free labour to the value of £100. Eriskay thus failed to obtain its breakwater, a facility which would have enabled the island to participate fully in the fishing boom at the time. The present jetty at Haun accommodates the ferry boat from Ludac. The jetty, constructed in recent years, is something of a disappointment to Eriskay. After years of waiting, and considering the money spent in its construction, the islanders could have expected a better piece of work. While it is of great service to small passenger craft, it offers nothing to larger ships. The island still awaits a deep-water berth for the cargo steamer.

The present interest of Eriskay in fishing has been helped by the Outer Hebrides Fisheries Training Scheme, now run by the Highlands and Islands Development Board. This scheme, first introduced by the Government in 1960, offered free training to men who were prepared to make fishing their career, together with financial assistance to those who satisfactorily completed their training and who wished to acquire boats of their own. The scheme was supported by finance for deposits on boats by the MacAulay (Rhodesia) Trust (which in 1959 had provided the initial impetus) and the Highland Fund Ltd, any balance being met by grants from Treasury sources. Through the scheme Eriskay acquired a boat equipped for dual-purpose fishing—ring-net during the normal herring season and nephrops trawling at other times. The present island fleet comprises six boats manned by thirty-two fishermen, and two small boats engaged in lobster fishing. The average gross yearly earnings of the fleet are about £80,000 (net earnings around £45,000), giving a high level of prosperity to a community that was in the past heavily dependent on employment in the Merchant Navy.

There is sea communication with South Uist and Barra, the main link being a motorboat ferry across the Sound of Eriskay to Ludac in South Uist. The 1967 Report of the Highland Transport Board recommended that the present small vessel be superseded by a vehicle ferry of the landing-craft type. Though there are only a handful of vehicles on Eriskay's 2 mile road, such a vessel would enable large and bulky goods and livestock to be conveyed to the island much more easily than at present. This vessel could also link South Uist (Lochboisdale), Eriskay and Barra in a more efficient and socially desirable manner than does the present MacBrayne's service between Castlebay in Barra and Lochboisdale, which ungallantly by-passes the smaller island. The new type of ferry service would also bring Barra within the area of benefits now obtainable from the Skye–North Uist vehicular ferry service.

During the 1940s the ferry between Ludac and Haun was subsidised by the GPO for carrying mails. In recent years, however, a Gilbertian situation arose. The mailboat left South Uist for Eriskay with mail on Mondays but did not take any off; but on Tuesdays it crossed to the island to take mail off, and did not bring any; and this pattern continued on alternate working days each week. It took the Member of Parliament for the Western Isles, Donald Stewart, to bring the matter to a sufficiently high level before a daily mail service to and from Eriskay was introduced.

The Eriskay Post Office was opened in November 1885. There was a mails delivery once each week. In an effort to improve communications and to direct the attention of the matter to the Congested Districts Board, Parliament was told, as an instance of the degree of isolation of the people of Eriskay, that they did not know of the death of Queen Victoria until 9 days after the event. A telegraph office was established on the island in 1902.

There is at present one school (Junior Secondary) on Eriskay, with about 50 pupils and three teachers. About a century ago one of the island's early schools was supported and assisted by the Free Church Ladies' Association, even though the entire population of Eriskay was of the Roman Catholic faith. It is on record that no religious difficulty arose from this provision and the parents were only too glad to have the opportunity of sending their children to obtain a rudimentary education.

Eriskay is attached to South Uist for administrative purposes and is administered by the County of Inverness-shire. Politically, the island forms part of the Western Isles Constituency.

Eriskay has always adhered to the old faith of the Hebrides. The present Catholic church was built at the turn of the century, after the original building had fallen into disrepair and when it had become too small to hold the swelling population. The prime mover behind the new building was Fr Allan MacDonald, whose main claim to fame is as a poet and folklorist, though he is better known and still remembered in the Southern Hebrides for his unfailing attention to his flock, which led to his death in 1905 at the age of forty-six. To help raise money for the new building, the Eriskay fishermen offered a day's fishing, and that particular day yielded the best catch of the season, worth £280. The funds for the church were also swelled by gifts from a Russian Jew, born in Paris and later resident in Edinburgh, who had heard of the island's needs. The church was opened in May 1903.

The building has since been altered and renovated, and the present church, St Michael's of the Sea, is a small and simple building in stone, with a curiously rounded gable pointed into the north-west wind. This design is similar to those found in Spain and in the Camargue—in Spain it is the custom to point rounded gables into the prevailing mistral—and was most probably derived from Fr Allan's stay in the old Scots College at Valladolid. The foundation is derived from the Parish of St Peter's in Daliburgh, South Uist.

The building holds a unique altarpiece. Some years ago a lifeboat from the aircraft carrier *Hermes*, washed overboard while the ship was engaged in exercises off St Kilda, came ashore at Pollachar in South Uist and was retrieved in a damaged condition; the bow, however, was cut off and fitted into the sanctuary of St Michael's of the Sea as the base for an altar. The altar table was secured on top and two anchors were fitted as further support. The resulting altarpiece is reminiscent of the pulpit in Melville's *Moby Dick*, and is eminently fitting for an island church.

Up until the turn of the present century the housing on Eriskay was much the same as elsewhere in the Hebrides and on the west coast of the Scottish mainland—leaving much to be desired, particularly from the viewpoint of sanitation. In 1891 the Sanitary Inspector of the County of Inverness reported that out of 459 houses in South Uist and in Eriskay, 70 per cent housed cattle under the same roof as the family.

Almost all the houses on Eriskay were improved in a short time by two circumstances. The first was the construction of the West Highland Railway in the early 1890s, on which a number of young men from the island were employed as navvies. They learned the use of crowbars and how to blast rocks, and on their return to Eriskay turned their new knowledge to good advantage. Instead of gathering suitably sized stones for new houses, they blasted good strong building stone from the island's hillsides. The other circumstance favouring housing improvement was a few consecutive seasons of very good fishing catches, particularly during 1900 and 1901, when the herring taken brought over £700 to the island. Between 1890 and 1900 some forty new houses were built. Ten of these were of stone and lime with gables and chimneys, and with roofs of tarred felt or corrugated iron. Cattle were banished to specially built out-houses or to the old black houses left deserted for the new buildings.

The new housing conditions largely removed the threat of disease that was ever present in the old houses. In 1896 there was a serious outbreak of typhus, particularly difficult to overcome because of the lack of any proper means of treatment; though even had the medical service been adequate, the sufferers' insanitary and overcrowded conditions would have prevented any success.

There was no hospital accommodation in the Hebrides for infectious diseases, and, indeed, such a provision would have been difficult. The Medical Officer for Inverness-shire asked, 'On which of the forty-nine inhabited islands are the hospitals to be erected?' His own suggestions were an improvement in Eriskay's housing or the provision of a mobile hospital. While he was reporting to his superiors, the incidence of the typhus epidemic increased. J. P. Day said: 'The people, panic-stricken, fled from the infected and left them to the care of a few devoted men led by the doctor and the priest. Nineteen deaths, including that of the priest, Fr George Rigg, occurred in 4 months.'

This epidemic was the subject of an inquiry by the Local Government Board, whose outcome was the dismissal of the local sanitary inspector and a call on the District Committee to provide, furnish and maintain a hospital for infectious diseases. The eventual provision was the conversion of a large building at Daliburgh on South Uist into a modest hospital, serviced by nurses obtained from Edinburgh. Today there is a resident district nurse on Eriskay, and doctors from South Uist cross the ferry to answer any urgent calls. Otherwise island patients are transferred to Daliburgh, where they are cared for by nuns.

The present houses on Eriskay are well built, with some features of modern design. Almost 90 per cent of the buildings have electricity, which is generated at the power station at Loch Carnan, South Uist, and carried by submarine cable to the island.

Eriskay formerly belonged to the MacNeils of Barra, but in 1758 the island, with other property, was disponed to a member of the Uist MacDonald family. It subsequently passed into the hands of John Gordon of Cluny, on whose death Lady Gordon Cathcart became proprietrix. She was in fact an absentee landlord, dying in 1935. In 1944 the trustees of her estate sold the island to a London banker, Herman Andrae.

One welcome visitor, which did not quite make it to the island, was the 12,000 ton cargo ship *Politician*, registered at Liverpool. She went aground off Calvay at the eastern inlet of the Sound of Eriskay in February 1941, when the navigator supposedly mistook the Eriskay Sound for the Sound of Barra. Her cargo included 24,000 cases of whisky for the American market. The crew were taken off safely and with them came the news of the ship's cargo. It was a windfall, in a time of wartime scarcity, which was bruited abroad throughout the Hebrides and the western seaboard of Scotland. Soon cases of whisky were being taken off the wreck and distributed far and wide. For their efforts, some men were brought up before the Sheriff at Lochmaddy Court and sentenced to terms of imprisonment of up to 2 months for offences against the excise laws. The incident provided the plot for the book and the film *Whisky Galore!*, by Sir Compton Mackenzie. The wreck was later cut in two; the fore part was towed to Rothesay, but the after end still lies under the waters of Eriskay Sound.

The Eriskay community today is strong and healthy, having seemingly won many of its battles, one of which was to get a new community hall, recently erected. The building will act as a focal point for the islanders.

With the new-found accessibility brought by the vehicular ferries across the Minch, an increasing number of tourists are finding a visit to Eriskay a high spot on their itinerary. Certainly the island in high summer presents an attraction which, coupled with the Eriskay 'myth' fostered by Mrs Kennedy Fraser, is rarely resisted.

The island has been, and to some extent still is, a fertile ground for folklorists and song-collectors. Fr Allan MacDonald, who spent the last 12 years of his short life as parish priest on the island, made a large collection of such items. The island's traditions have been preserved mainly through the efforts of Dr John Lorne Campbell of Canna, who has spent many years in publishing Fr MacDonald's work. His collection reflects the way of life and Gaelic-based cultural background of Eriskay and the Hebrides in general.

To the south of Eriskay lie the Stack Islands, on the largest of which, Eilean Leathan, stands Weaver's Castle, a small fort

140ft above sea level which once belonged to the MacNeils of Barra and was used for piratical purposes. The walls are made of small stones cemented with lime. John MacCulloch says of it: 'On Eriska, there is a tower which has been a stronghold of the Mac Neils: though small, it is striking, from the scarcity of art in this doleful country.'

7   VATERSAY

VATERSAY is an unusual Siamese-twin island with a head and a body, both well defined. They are joined together by a low isthmus of sandy hillocks, with a bay on each side of it. That on the west side, Bagh Siar, is sandy near its head. Vatersay Bay, on the east, looks to Muldoanich Island, some 2 miles out into the Minch. The northern part of Vatersay is about $3\frac{1}{2}$ miles long, running roughly from west to east, and about a mile across. The highest point is Heishaval Mor (625ft), which is attended by its neighbour Heishaval Beag (615ft). Towards the east of this part of Vatersay runs a promontory comprising Uidh and Creag Mor. Uidh faces Castlebay in Barra across about $1\frac{1}{2}$ miles of tidal water which can be very rough at times. The Sound of Vatersay to the north of the island separates it from the southern coast of Barra.

The southern part of Vatersay is about 2 miles west–east and reaches a height of 279ft in Ben Rulibreck. Am Meall, a high cliff at the southern end of Vatersay Bay is 327ft and rises steeply from the sea. The southern end of this part of Vatersay has a sandy-headed bay called Bagh a' Deas.

There are no roads, but there is an efficient network of good tracks totalling 5 miles. These extend from Coalis in the north, westwards to Uidh, and southwards to the Vatersay township on the south part of the island, near Vatersay Bay. There are six vans and a lorry on the island.

The four townships (Coalis, Uidh, Vatersay and Eorisdale) contain new and neat-looking houses, spaced rather hap-

167

hazardly. Fairly high fields offer grazing for cows on their lower slopes and for sheep on higher reaches.

Vatersay has three ancient brochs or duns. One lies near the main township of Vatersay. The ruins of a second lie at Coalis (Dun a' Chaolais, the Fort of the Strait), and the third is on the rock-islet of Biruaslum, a high and virtually inaccessible stack west of Vatersay.

To the east of the Uidh promontory lies the tidal islet of Uinessan, which has the ancient burial ground and ruined church of Cille Bhrianain. The chapel is commonly called Caibeal Moire nan Ceann, the Chapel of Mary of the Heads, a reference to a woman from the island of Coll in the Inner Hebrides who married one of the MacNeils of Barra; she had an unpleasant nature, being feared for her hasty temper and momentary flashes of cruelty, and her practice was to remove the heads of anyone who crossed her.

Vatersay has been inhabited for many centuries and still supports a population closely geared to life and conditions on neighbouring Barra. In 1794 there were two farms. The population in 1861 was thirty-two, which later dropped to thirteen in 1901. But it had risen by the 1911 Census to 288, through migration from the overcrowded island of Barra and the desertion of nearby Mingulay. The population in 1931 was 240, falling to 151 by 1951. The 1965 intercensal return showed a population of ninety, and today there are about seventy.

The island has a sub post office, school, chapel, and public telephone box. External communications by sea consist of an irregular ferry operating between Vatersay and Castlebay in Barra.

The economy of Vatersay has always been land-based. That it was a fertile island is evidenced by a note in 1886 that it supported 1,200 cattle and 400 sheep. Lobster fishing, which now provides a reasonable source of income, has never constituted more than a small element in the island's economy. Herring fishing touched Vatersay only peripherally. In 1868

James Methuen, a leading Scottish fish-curer and a pioneer of deep-sea herring fishing, sank capital into the development of a large class of boats known as the 'Anstruther Build'. These craft were more than successful and contributed largely to the general increase in the economic wealth of the Outer Hebrides based on herring. Methuen chose Castlebay in Barra as a centre for fish-curing, and its natural harbour was often chock-full with drifters. Vatersay Bay acted as an overspill harbour, but the benefit to the island was negligible.

During the first decade of this century events outside Vatersay raised the population to almost 300 in the space of a couple of years. This is what happened.

At the turn of the century Vatersay was an island farm, occu-pied by one farmer and his family, as tenants of Lady Gordon Cathcart. The conditions in Barra and on South Uist, both the property of Lady Cathcart, were congested, to say the least. Land-hungry crofters were agitating for room to move, to live and to make their living. The estate management did what it thought best to relieve the situation, which arose largely through the erection of additional dwellings in existing townships by squatters. These erections were mere huts, often built overnight.

Twenty years previously, Lady Cathcart had promoted emigration schemes to relieve the congestion, but incurred such heavy losses that she discontinued them. By 1901 the position was very bad. In that year the Government, under what it chose to call 'excessive pressure', bought 3,000 acres in Barra and gave fifty-eight crofters new holdings; but this still left nearly half of the landless cottars, or squatters, unprovided for. Congestion was particularly acute around Castlebay, from which in 1902 several cottars applied to the Congested Districts Board for ground on Vatersay for planting potatoes. Vatersay and its adjoining island constituted the only farm then left on the Barra estate, but the tenant's terms proved too high for an immediate acceptance by the Board.

In the following year, however, the Board managed to buy

60 acres on Uidh (Vatersay island) for £600 and an annual feu duty of 10s. The 60 acres were divided among fifty-one cottars, who planted potato seed but failed to obtain satisfactory crops. In 1905 the Board, wishing to find out the reason for the crop failure, proposed to carry out tests on the soil, but the cottars opposed this move and became decidedly restless. They claimed they did not know whether the Board would allow them to sow oats and barley on the potato land, or whether it was worth their while starting to collect seaweed for any further land that might be provided. There was also the prospect of a coming winter season without potatoes. Early in 1906 negotiations for fresh land on Uidh were opened, but almost broke down. The tenant asked 10s an acre for the lease of a new patch of land of some 20 acres. The Board refused the offer on the grounds that it was too high and in any case they did not believe that their original purchase was so useless for potato-growing.

Matters came to a head. The cottars threatened that they would take the land they needed by force. The Board then climbed down and rented the 20 acres, stipulating that potatoes were to be cropped in 1906 and corn in the following year.

Hoping that things would settle down, the Board was more than taken by surprise on hearing that on 19 August 1906 one of the cottars had flitted from Castlebay to where the main Vatersay township is now situated and erected a wooden dwelling with the help of a few willing friends. The house was up and thatched in a few hours and a fire lit. It is an old law in Scotland that if a house can be erected, roofed and fired between sunrise and sunset on the same day, the houseowner can take possession of the land. In 1907 six other cottars from Castlebay and Mingulay followed their leader and took up residence on Vatersay. They stocked their claims with cattle and sheep. Lady Gordon Cathcart's estate managers had no option but to prepare complaints for breach of interdict. In July 1907 the Secretary for Scotland sent a sheriff to try to induce the people to withdraw their cattle (now grazing on the Vatersay farm lands) and to abandon their illegal conduct, but he failed to persuade the squatters to leave, and withdrew, suggesting that the best possible solution might be for the Congested Districts Board to buy the whole island.

The following year saw the Vatersay raiders brought to trial in Edinburgh and each sentenced to 6 months' imprisonment. But the whole affair raised such a public outcry that they were given an early release.

It was suggested to Lady Cathcart that she should co-operate in the formation of new holdings in Vatersay. In reply she said that she did not think the island suitable for new holdings because the water supply was insufficient. In addition, the raiders were not suitable tenants, nor was she willing to face the contingent liabilities in the way of rates for a new school, or the provision of adequate water. There was the extra burden of paying compensation to a farming tenant she did not wish to remove. In the end, in 1909, the Board announced that it was making arrangements to buy Vatersay with its farm (2,278 acres, apart from the 60 acres on Uidh) for £6,250 and to pay the sitting tenant compensation for his removal. Fifty-eight holdings were formed, for which eighty-three applications were received. Fifty-eight tenants were selected and proceedings taken to have the remainder of the squatters removed. The rental for Vatersay totalled £157 for the island's land area, plus the neighbouring islands of Sandray, Flodday, Lingay, Biruaslum and Greanamul (a total of 1,178 acres).

The Board resolved that the settlement should be confined to Vatersay only and that it should consist of holdings suitable for the accommodation of crofter-fishermen. A limit of sixty holdings was imposed; the original fifty-eight holdings were divided between the four townships of Coalis (16), Uidh (14), Vatersay (20) and Eorisdale (8) on the south-east tip of the island. The Board had to undertake, at a cost of some £1,300, various works of adaptation, such as roads, fences, drainage and a water supply for each township and its livestock.

The present community numbers about seventy crofter-fishermen and their families on sixty-four crofts. The island is included in the improvement schemes of the Inverness-shire Water Board, which intends providing an undersea water main from the south end of Barra across Vatersay Sound. Engineers of the 36th Engineer Regiment have made a survey of the seabed of the Sound. About 60 per cent of the houses are connected to mains electricity under the Rural Development Scheme of the North of Scotland Hydro-electric Board. The supply is at present generated at the diesel generating station at Loch Carnan on South Uist.

The community is alive, with a real sense of purpose. There are individual farming projects and prospects of building up a small lobster fleet. The island has a significant export in cattle, the beasts swimming across Vatersay Sound to Barra, whence they are taken to Oban on one of MacBrayne's boats. The cattle swim has been an annual event for more than half a century, but it results in the cattle reaching the Oban sales in poor condition. The cattle are tied to a long painter fixed to the stern of a dinghy towed by a motorboat. They are then towed, four at a time, across the channel, men taking up positions beside them to ensure that their heads stay above the water.

About six crofters on the island have built up a stock of over 100 cattle of the Aberdeen-Angus, Shorthorn and Hereford breeds. The annual value of the exported cattle is around £3,500.

The island school roll was twenty-six in 1955, but only nine 10 years later. After children reach the age of eleven they leave Vatersay to attend Castlebay Junior Secondary School. There is neither doctor nor nurse on Vatersay, medical services being provided from Barra.

In 1813 Vatersay was the scene of the wreck of the *Annie Jane*, bound for America out of Liverpool with a cargo of over 500 'redemptioners'. This was the term given to emigrants who booked passages that were to be paid for by instalments out of their earnings when they got to the other side. Twice the *Annie Jane* had to return to Liverpool because of bad weather. The third time some headway was made, but the ship was forced north and found herself off Vatersay. She ran aground and broke up on the reefs on the west coast. More than 450 bodies were washed ashore. It was a tragedy with an irony, for many of those who perished came from the Outer Hebrides. Instead of finding a new life in a new land, they found death on the rocks of their home shores.

8   THE SMALL ISLANDS

ALL the main islands of the Southern Hebrides are attended by small satellites, ranging from the larger habitable islands to small grass-covered islets. In their time these small islands have fulfilled both social and economic functions. Today they are largely extensions of the common grazing areas of the crofting townships on the main islands, or are rented by tenants for grazing sheep. The offshore islands that have retained their population are generally within good communicating distances of their associated larger islands. Some islands, however, were populated only because they afforded a temporary refuge from the clearances which took place in Harris, the Uists and Barra, the displaced islanders preferring to remain on a nearby island than to face the unknown in places such as North America. Hellisay is a case in point, its population of 108 in 1841 falling to seven in the next 10 years through emigration to nearby Eriskay.

In the Hebridean chain some five islands per decade have lost their populations since 1841. The process of desertion continues. Only the very large islands remain populated, though the populations of most of them are falling. Social rather than economic reasons are behind it. The need for social intercourse has increased during the past century. Where and when it was not satisfied, desertion followed. The small islands in this chapter are only a few of many in the Hebrides whose stories are sadly similar.

VALLAY

The low-lying tidal island of Vallay fits snugly into a large shallow sand bight off the north-west coast of North Uist. Access to Vallay is by way of a foot-track across the sands of Vallay Strand, the ford which runs between Claddach Vallay on the main island and Vallay House. The strand dries out at low water. The island is roughly 2 miles long and about a mile wide. It is composed of sand based on a rock bed, mostly covered with grass, and its highest point is Ceann Uachdarach (126ft).

To the west of Vallay lie the remains of a forest of trees which can be seen at low spring tides, evidence that the Outer Hebrides were once covered with woodland and scrub. This submerged forest is the result of Holocene sinkings, which allowed the rapid advance of the shell-sand beaches. Erskine Beveridge (who visited North Uist in 1897) noted that he had often seen tree trunks and branches lying in peat at a level about 12ft below highwater mark. Some of these trunks had diameters up to 14in, and were apparently birch. There is a bay called Bagh nan Craobhag (Bay of Small Trees).

There is a sulphur well in the marsh to the west of Vallay Loch. On the southern side of the island stands Vallay House and its farm buildings.

The first recorded occupant of Vallay was Godfrey Mac-Gorrie, who held it around 1516. In the eighteenth century the tack of Vallay was held by members of the family of MacLean. The old House of Vallay was built in 1742 by Ewen MacDonald, and was one of four slated houses noted in the Parish of North Uist in 1794. Ewen MacDonald was a son of Major William MacDonald of Aird, in Skye, tutor to the heir of MacDonald of Sleat. Various possessors of tacks after the middle of the eighteenth century appear in the records. One of these was the Minister of North Uist, the Rev Finlay MacRae, who contributed the article 'North Uist' to the *New Statistical Account*,

1837. Vallay was sold by Baron MacDonald to Erskine Beveridge of Dunfermline in 1901. It is now part of the North Uist estate of Lord Granville.

In 1851 the population was two men only, but by 1861 it had risen to fifty-six, afterwards falling to forty-three and then nineteen by 1921 and 1931 respectively. Documentary evidence exists of the island's use as farmland around 1620. Oral evidence given before the Royal Commission on Crofting (taken in 1883) indicated a clearance of the resident population in the decades 1820–50. The population reached its peak of fifty-nine in 1841. Vallay is still inhabited by a farming family.

BORERAY

Boreray is a small, roughly oval island of about $4\frac{1}{2}$ miles in circumference, lying about a mile north-east of the tip of the North Uist peninsular sand-shelf which ends in Ard a' Mhorain. The island reaches a height of 176ft in the flattish summit of Mullach Mor to the north. The southern part of the island is flat and is about 50ft above sea level. Boreray is bounded by steep sandhills on the south-eastern side, while the western and northern coasts are shelving cliffs, with offshore rocks and shoals. There are remains of standing stones and chapels.

Boreray village lies in a bay on the eastern side of the island; a small stream runs through the village area. A large loch on the eastern side of Boreray, Loch Mor, becomes brackish when the sea breaks over the narrow strip of land separating it from the sea.

Boreray is a fertile island. In 1845 thirty families were recorded as 'living in comfort', in 1851 the population was 158 and in 1855 it was 160. The peak had been reached in 1841 with 181. By 1921 the population had declined to sixty-three and it had fallen to seven in 1951 (three males and four females). One family is still resident on Boreray.

The island must have been inhabited in the late fifteenth

century and early sixteenth, for some coins of James IV's reign were found in a sandhill in 1836.

During the years 1922–3 the island was evacuated at the request of its seventeen tenants, one of whom decided at the eleventh hour to stay behind and so fell heir to a croft of some 87 acres. The remainder of Boreray was let as grazing to crofters on the neighbouring island of Berneray. The tenants who left Boreray ultimately found themselves with crofts on the main island of North Uist with no road access to the rest of the island and with less acreage of arable land than they had on Boreray. There the crofters had had an average of 24 acres of arable land, in fixed and shifting runrig (strip farming), and about 350 acres of common pasture, including 10 acres on the nearby small island of Lingay. The latter island also supplied Boreray's peat.

Over-cultivation in the nineteenth century caused serious deterioration of the land on Boreray. According to evidence given to the Royal Commission on Crofting in 1883, for every 5 bushels sown the crofters reaped only 10. The reason given for the decline was that in 1810 the tacksman on Boreray had left, and with him went the main source of initiative on which the islanders had come to depend. The island's pier fell into disrepair and landing was made difficult. The islanders then became fearful that Boreray would be swept away by a great storm. Ultimately, in the contemporary climate of crofter resettlement in the Hebrides during the 1920s, the Boreray crofters were evacuated. The family which remained on the island is still reaping the benefits of its last-minute decision—and has to date not been blown away by a great storm!

Martin Martin tells the story of a Dutchman, Captain Peters, who sheltered his ship in the lee of Boreray in the late seventeenth century. One of his crew ventured ashore and came across ten women employed 'in a strange manner'. This was in fact one of the earliest descriptions of waulking or thickening hand-made cloth of the type now known as Harris Tweed.

L

Martin also records: 'In the middle of this Island, there's a Fresh-water Lake, well stock'd with very big Eels, some of them as long as Cod, or Ling-fish; there is a passage under the Stony Ground, which is between the Sea and the Lake, through which it's suppos'd the Eels come in with the Spring Tides; one of the Inhabitants called Mack-Vanish, i.e. Monks-son, had the curiosity to creep naked through this Passage.'

The inhabitants of Boreray used to pasture their lambs upon a neighbouring islet called Eilean nan Uan until it was entirely washed away in the eighteenth century. It is now represented by a shoal known as Oitir nan Uan.

RONAY

Ronay island, with the larger Grimsay, lies in the wide rock-and-sand channel dividing Benbecula from North Uist. Its eastern coast faces into the Minch. It is a large rugged island with an extremely indented rocky coastline. It virtually consists of a series of steep hills, comparatively bare to the north but heather-clad towards the south. There are two high points —Beinn a' Charnain (379ft) and Beinn Rodagrich (325ft). The smaller portion of Ronay, Ronaybeg, is joined to the rest of the island by an isthmus 400yd wide.

Ronay had a large population at one time. In the *Moral Statistics Report* of the Gaelic School Society (1826) it is recorded that 180 people lived on the island, but they were cleared off about 1831. Many went to the neighbouring island of Grimsay. The population recorded in 1841 was nine, and by 1861 it was only four (two males, two females). Each subsequent census decade showed five or six people until 1931. The island is at present let to a North Uist farmer for grazing some 300 sheep, and the Spanish Ambassador in London has a house there. Otherwise it is uninhabited.

Martin Martin notes 'a little Chappel in the Island Rona, called the *Low-landers* Chappel, because Seamen who dye in time of Fishing, are buried in that place'. This is apparently a reference to a pre-Reformation chapel. A rocky knoll near the west side of Ronay is known as Cnoc nan Gall, a name referring in some measure to strangers or lowlanders.

WIAY

The island of Wiay lies off the south-east corner of Benbecula. Its shape is roughly rectangular with a tapering peninsula ending in Rubha Cam nan Gall. The highest point on the island is Beinn a Tuath (334ft); it has a thick covering of heather and rough pasturage, with few protruding rocks, and slopes gently all round. The old settlement on Wiay lies over to the western side of the island facing the mouth of Loch Leiravagh in Benbecula.

Wiay had a recorded population of six (2 males, 4 females) in 1861, and of four (3 males, 1 female) in 1901, since when it has been uninhabited. Near Wiay is a tiny islet of Eileann na Cille, which returned, for the first and only time, a population of four persons in 1951.

MONACH ISLANDS

The Monachs and their associated rocks are fully described in the companion book in the *Islands* Series: *St Kilda and Other Hebridean Outliers*. They are a group of low-lying islands some 5 miles south-west of Hougharry Point in North Uist. There are five islands, three of which are joined together at low water by exposed shallow sandy beaches. Unlike many other Hebridean islands, the Monachs are unusual in that they are less than 50ft above sea level. The three main islands are Ceann Ear (East Head), Shivinish, and Ceann Iar (West Head). The two smaller islands are Shillay, now the site of a deserted lighthouse, and Stockay.

The islands have a history of human settlement going back

before AD 1000. One of the earliest references to them concerns the establishment of a nunnery, attached to Iona, on Ceann Ear. A monastery on Shillay was erected on the site of the now deserted lighthouse, and it was part of the monks' duties to maintain a light as a navigational guide to mariners sailing in the nearby western Atlantic waters. The religious associations of the Monachs came to an end after the Reformation.

In 1595 the islands were said to be able to raise twenty men of military age, suggesting a total population of about 100 people. In 1764 the population was seventy. About 1810 the population was entirely removed, the result of a complete failure of the soil. The records of the period point to over-grazing, which exposed large areas of sand. This erosion was worsened by a great storm which tore up the remaining turf and covered all the islands with worthless sand. Later, marram grass was planted, and that stabilised the soil sufficiently to enable the land to be used again by a returning population. In 1861 the population was 127 and it reached its maximum in 1891 at 135. By the turn of the century the population had begun a decline that continued: 1914, about eighty; 1921, sixty-six; 1931, thirty-three; 1932, two families, who left in 1942. Since then the islands have been deserted.

They were well served with amenities, provided by various agencies. There was a post office, and a school that was maintained by Church bodies until 1874, when it was taken over by the School Board. There was no shop, but the islanders' spiritual wants were supplied by a missionary.

The Monach Isles are now occasionally visited by lobster fishermen, who lodge in those houses which still remain in a reasonable state of repair.

FUDAY

The island of Fuday lies in the Sound of Barra. The name has two derivations: (1) from the Gaelic Fuideidh—an island lying by itself apart from other islands; and (2) Old Norse: Utey—outside isle.

Fuday rises in three hills, the central and highest being Mullach Neachel at 294ft. The island is covered with grass and a stream of good water flows into Cordale Beag, a small indent in the coastline on the southern end. Cordale Mor, on the eastern side, is a well defined sandy bay. On the western side is Traigh na Reill, a sand-based shelf. The north-western coast of Fuday rises in high sandhills, and the western extreme of the island, Dunan Ruadh, is a sandy point.

Walker's list for 1764 does not mention Hellisay island, but gives a population of fifty-six for 'Fuda'; but by 1841 Hellisay had 108 while Fuday had only five. It is possible that Walker's 'Fuda' was in fact Hellisay, since in Gaelic it was sometimes known as 'An t-eilean Fuideach'. Fuday had a population of five in 1841, seven in 1861 (4 males, 3 females), six in 1881, seven in 1891 and four in 1901 (2 males, 2 females), since when it has been deserted.

There is a tradition that the island was once used by Norsemen as their burial ground. Their graves can still be seen in the sand, built of rounded stones. In Norse times it was necessary to find a quiet island for the dead to rest in peace.

Another tradition makes Fuday the last retreat of those Norsemen who remained after their power had been broken at the Battle of Largs in 1263. An illegitimate son of MacNeil of Barra fell in love with one of the Norse maids and she with him. But his love was more calculating than real. Through her he gained knowledge of the Norse defences, and, to establish his position within his father's household, he led a raid on Fuday and wiped out the islanders. Hence the Norse graves.

GIGHAY

Gighay, with its close neighbour Hellisay, lies at the southern end of the Sound of Barra, where it enters the Minch. It is roughly triangular in shape and reaches a height of 305ft at Mullach a' Charnain. An Laogh (the Calf) is a point of rock 24ft high and separated from Gighay's main mass by a narrow channel. Meall an Laogh (Calf Lump), in the north-eastern part of Gighay, is a high flat rising terminating in a hummock. The eastern side of this extremity is very steep. The island's name is thought to be derived from 'Gydha's Isle' (Gydha was a woman's name in Old Norse).

Dean Monro recorded that Gighay was inhabited in 1549, but there are no other details or records of its inhabitants. It was also noted as supporting a population at the end of the eighteenth century. It is now deserted.

HELLISAY

The island of Hellisay lies just south of Gighay at the entrance of Barra Sound into the Minch. It is about 1½ miles long and about ½ mile across. The island has two distinct peaks—Meall More, near the south-eastern end reaching 241ft, and Ben a' Charnain (242ft), in the north-west. The former has a vertical face of some 200ft to the west which has distinct range markings near the top from its lichen vegetation. The island name is derived from Old Norse meaning Cave's Isle.

Its population reached its height in 1841, with 108 persons, and like some other islands its population rose with a temporary influx of people evicted from the main islands nearby. The number in 1764 was fifty-six. After 1841 it declined rapidly, to seven in 1851, twenty in 1861, and nine in 1881. It has been deserted since 1891.

MULDOANICH

Muldoanich is a round island about ½ mile in diameter, steep and hogbacked with craggy cliffs and a maximum height of 505ft. It stands outside the line of the Barra satellite islands,

2 miles east of Vatersay. Dean Monro records that the island had once a chapel, which one would expect from the derivation of the island's name: in Gaelic, it is *Maol Domhnaich*, 'the island of the tonsured one of the Lord'. MacCulloch, however, offers an incorrect but interesting derivation of Muldoanich from St Duncan, who was reckoned to be a person of considerable importance in the Highlands and Islands of Scotland, where Sunday is known as Di Donich, Duncan's Day.

To the north-west of the island are some ragged rocks appropriately called Sgeirean Fiaclach (tooth rocks).

The pyramidal bugle has been found by botanists on the island.

SANDRAY

Sandray (sandy) island lies ½ mile south of Vatersay. It is a large round island about 1½ miles in diameter and over 1,000 acres in extent. The centre of the island rises to 678ft at Cairn Galtar. There are two good streams and a small loch. In Monro's time the island was 'inhabit and manurit', and it supported no less than nine farms in 1794.

MacCulloch records: 'Nearly connected with Vatersay, with which it corresponds in materials and disposition; forming a single hill of gneiss . . . At a distance the island appears as if covered with a coating of snow.' This snowy look is caused by sand covering the west side of the island to such a height that it looks like a white hill. There is a dun high up on Cairn Galtar overlooking the Atlantic, and there are faint traces of an old chapel site, Cille Bhride (Bride's Cell), now partly occupied by a sheep-dipping tank. The island's grazings form part of the crofting common holdings of Vatersay, and abound with rabbits.

Hazels have been recorded.

In 1861 Sandray had a population of nine (2 males, 7 females), 20 years later it was 10, and in 1901 only three. After that date there was a temporary influx of evicted people, raising the population to forty-one in 1911. In 1930 the last record of population returned a figure of twenty, but by 1934 the island had been deserted.

PABBAY

Pabbay island is one of many Hebridean islands so called. The name is derived from the Gaelic: Pabaidh—Priest's Isle. It is separated from Mingulay by the 2 mile wide Sound of Mingulay. The island is about 2 miles long east to west by about a mile wide. The highest point is The Hoe (560ft), at the south-west corner of the island, where there are also some very high sea cliffs. The east side of Pabbay is a gradual slope, and near the east shore a large mass of blown sand rises to a height of about 250ft. The shell-sand on Pabbay is extremely rich in lime, so rich in fact that the frequent rains have resulted in the break-down of the sand to produce beds of impure limestone.

On the east side of Pabbay also a peninsula, Rosinish, juts dramatically into the waters of the Minch, across a natural sea-made arch. The point, which rises to a height of 133ft, is long, bare, rough and rocky. At the junction of Pabbay with its promontory lies the Red Fort, Dunan Ruadh, a broch which looks across the Sound of Pabbay to the dun on Sandray. At Bagh Ban (White Bay) there are traces of a chapel. Drifting sands have uncovered human bones, perhaps evidence that the chapel once had an associated burial ground. Three cross-marked stones are also to be seen; a fourth rather interesting stone is marked with a crescent, a cross and a lily. These symbols are not in the usual run of traditional carvings and are of a quite different character to the more common interlacing patterns found on stone-work in the Outer Hebrides. It has been suggested that these unusual markings have some connection with the eastern 'Pictish' parts of north and north-east Scotland.

Martin Martin observed of Pabbay: 'The natives observe

that if six sheep are put a-grazing in the little island of Pabbay, five of them still appear fat, but the sixth a poor skeleton, but any number in this island not exceeding five are always very fat.' It does not appear that Martin visited most of the smaller islands around Barra, for his map shows Pabbay and Mingulay in each other's positions.

The remains of the old township settlement can be seen on the east of the island.

In 1794 the population of Pabbay included three farming families, making up some twenty people. In 1861 the population was fourteen, in 1881 its maximum of twenty-six, in 1901 eleven, and in 1911 seven; since then the island has been deserted.

MINGULAY

The island of Mingulay is separated from Berneray by the ½ mile wide Sound of Berneray. It is about 2½ miles long and about 1½ across. The eastern coastline of Mingulay slopes gradually to the sea, but the western is more rugged. The island has four rounded summits, the highest of which are Carnan (891ft) and MacPhee's Hill (735ft). Mingulay Bay, a broad indentation on the east side of the island, has a sandy beach about ¼ mile long. The island's deserted village lies at the head of Mingulay Bay. Some of Mingulay's cliffs are breathtaking when viewed from seaward. The precipice of Aonaig and the rock-stacks of Arnamul and Lianamul are very fine. Harvie-Brown thought that the latter had the closest-packed guillemot station he had ever seen. Mingulay also supports a very large puffinry. Biulacraig, which is the second highest cliff in Britain, next to Conachair on St Kilda, rises a sheer 700ft from the Atlantic waters.

The island's name is derived from the Old Norse meaning 'Big Isle'. Its cliffs, however, have seemed to attract more comment than the island itself. Martin Martin mentions the stack of Lianamul on Mingulay's west side as

... almost inaccessible, except in one place, and that by climb-
ing, which is very difficult. This rock abounds with sea-fowls,
such as the guillemot, coulterneb, puffin, etc. The chief climber
is commonly called Gingich, and this name imports a big man
having strength and courage proportionable ... by the assistance of a rope of horsehair, he draws his fellows out of the boat
upon this high rock, and draws the rest up after him with the
rope, till they arrive at the top.

The *Old Statistical Account* also mentions Lianamul, the top of
which was covered with grass, and adds that the Mingulay
people climbed to the top of it 'at the risk of their lives, and
by means of a rope carry up their wedders to fatten'.

Harvie-Brown mentions that Lianamul was once connected
to Mingulay by a rope bridge, cliff to cliff, but that this had
disappeared many years before his first visit in 1871. Records
indicate that Lianamul provided grazing for five sheep and the
more southerly stack of Arnamul for twenty sheep.

The stratification of Mingulay island is quite horizontal, a
feature which has given rise to its vertical cliffs with wide ledges,
both incut and overhung. In part of his evidence submitted to
the Crofters Commission in 1883, Alexander Carmichael said:

There is probably no more interesting island in Britain than this
island of Miuley, with its wonderful precipices, long narrow
sea galleries several hundred feet high in the perpendicular
sides, and marine arcades, winding their gloomy subterranean
ways under the precipitous island. To boat through these galleries
and arcades needs a calm sea, a good crew, and a steady nerve.
The writer was the first to discover and the first and last to go
through much of the longest, largest and gloomiest of these
wonderful sinuous sea arcades.

Neil Munro, author of *Children of the Tempest*, describes an
imaginary climb on the walls of one of Mingulay's sea cliffs.

There is evidence that Mingulay was settled very early in
the history of the Outer Hebrides. At the south-west corner of

Mingulay Bay is Crois an t-Suidheachain, a stone setting resembling part of a short stone cist, giving a possible link with the Bronze Age in Britain. The area round the cross was at one time regarded with some reverence by the islanders, who celebrated open-air masses in its vicinity. A number of other places on Mingulay have either traceable ruins of chapels and duns, or placenames indicating the existence of structures now completely disappeared.

In 1794 the island supported eight farms, with a population of about forty people, a slight decrease on the figure of fifty-two recorded for 1764. By 1861 the figure was thirty-nine, by 1865 eighty, and by 1866 seventy. The peak in Mingulay's population was recorded in 1881, at 150, after which there was a decline to 135 in 1901, eleven in 1911, four in 1931, and two in 1934. There have been none since. Almost the whole of the Mingulay population was transferred to Vatersay when that island was settled with crofters in 1909, only a handful remaining in the Mingulay township, which still stands in a surprisingly good state of repair. The island is now only occasionally frequented by a visiting shepherd.

T. S. Muir, writing in 1866, describes Mingulay village as 'a picturesque huddle of rude dusky huts, inhabited by 18 families, supporting themselves by their fishings, and the potatoes, small oats, rye, and barley, grown on their little farms. The rents of these, I was told, range from £2 10s. to £3 10s. each.' Muir goes on to say that each crofter kept two or three cows and at least one pony, and that they had plenty of peat. The island also supplied peat for the people on Berneray, who had none on their own island.

In Muir's time, some of the crofters, 'families of primitive people', helped support themselves by catching birds on the island's sea cliffs and gathering the birds' eggs, though this activity was of more economic significance in previous centuries. Rent for Mingulay was paid to MacNeil of Barra in 'fachaich', the fatling young of the shearwater. MacNeil would arrive in

Mingulay Bay in his galley from Barra a fortnight before Lammas and remain on the island for 4 weeks. Until he arrived, the islanders were not allowed to hunt the shearwater. The yield was some twenty barrels each year. The crofts then were of different sizes: Peighinn (penny) crofts paid two barrels of fachaich per annum, Leth-peighinn (halfpenny) crofts paid one barrel, Feoirlig (farthing) crofts paid half a barrel, and Clitig (half-farthing) crofts paid a quarter-barrel.

Martin Martin relates that if any Mingulay man lost his wife it was customary for him to ask MacNeil of Barra to choose him another. A widow, in like manner, could apply for a husband. MacNeil also performed a social service in replacing any of his tenants' milking cows that might be lost in bad weather or by accident.

Alexander Carmichael, in further evidence of the social conditions of the Hebrideans presented to the Crofters Commission in 1883, writes:

> The people of Miuley do not seem to have used ropes as they do in St Kilda, but to have clambered among the rocks like goats. These rocks are wonderfully grand. Mr Campbell of Islay and the writer measured the highest of these in October 1871, when the barometer showed nearly 800 feet above the sea. The place is named Aonaig, and this particular rock is called Biolacraig. The face of the cliff is as smooth and perpendicular as the wall of a house, and goes sheer down into the Atlantic. This precipice was the crest of the ancient MacNeils of Bara, and 'Biolacraig' formed the rallying cry of the clan. There are a few of the tenants who are not much in arrear (of rents), but there are others who are very deeply in arrear. Calculating the whole, and comparing the gross amount of arrears and the gross amount of rent, there are upwards of five years' rent in arrears, and some of them are upwards of ten, for instance at Mingulay.

Mingulay supported a school in the 1880s, originally started by the Free Church Ladies' Association, later the Ladies' Highland Association.

In an issue of the *Inverness Courier* of 1866 a writer suggested converting the strait between Berneray and Mingulay into a harbour of refuge, by throwing a breakwater across the west end. This would have provided shipping and fishermen with an excellent harbour, but nothing came of the suggestion.

BERNERAY

Berneray (Old Norse: Bjorn's Isle) is the southernmost island of the Outer Hebridean chain and bears the Barra Head lighthouse, which towers 68oft out of the sea. The island is about $1\frac{1}{2}$ miles across by a mile deep, and is wedge-shaped, with an area of some 400 acres. It is 54 miles from the most westerly point of Scotland, Ardnamurchan Point, and 95 miles from the nearest point in Ireland. The beam of the lighthouse is visible for 35 miles and, in good weather, the island itself is visible from the top of Ben Nevis, some 100 miles away.

Berneray rises to a height of 628ft at Skate Point, which lifts itself sheer out of the sea. These cliffs, which swarm with seabirds, receive the full force of the Atlantic winds and waves, and some reports have stated that after severe gales small fish have been picked up on the grassy summits. In his *Scenery of Scotland* Sir Archibald Geikie records that 'on this island, during a storm in January 1836, a mass of gneiss containing 504 cubic ft, and estimated to be about 42 tons in weight, was gradually moved 5 ft from the place where it lay.' As a matter of interest, a force of 60,831lb/ft² was measured at Skerryvore, 36 miles to the south of Berneray, such was the strength and weight of the pounding Atlantic waves.

The island supports a large puffinry and grey seals make it one of their favourite Hebridean haunts. The soil, noted in the *New Statistical Account*, is of different kinds in different places: moss, light sand, light black soil and meadow land. There is a granite quarry which supplies the beautifully marked, fine quality stone of which the Barra Head lighthouse and its outbuildings are constructed.

The lighthouse is on the south-west point of the island, on a promontory close by an ancient dun or broch. The house is a 6oft high white tower that was erected in 1833. In 1840 the Commissioners of Northern Lighthouses used to employ a small vessel to ply between Barra Head lighthouse and Tobermoray with the monthly returns, as a quicker means of post than the route which then existed from North Uist to Dunvegan in Skye.

All that is left of the dun near the lighthouse is a stone wall across the neck of the promontory. It is built in the usual style associated with these structures, in thick set drystone with galleries running into it. A second fort called Dun Briste, lying a little to the north of the lighthouse, is also a promontory fort. On MacLean's point is the site of an old chapel and burial ground. A stone slab with an incised cross is the visible evidence of the chapel, which existed many centuries ago.

Three families are recorded living on Berneray in 1794. In 1861 the population was thirty-four, and this figure had risen to fifty-seven 20 years later. The population trend subsequently was 1886 forty, 1891 thirty-six, 1901 seventeen, 1911 five, 1921 ten, 1931 six, 1951 six, and 1961 three. In the later years the population comprised the lightkeepers only.

BIBLIOGRAPHY

BOOKS

ANDERSON, I. F. *Across Hebridean Seas* (1937)
ANDERSON, JAMES. *An Account of the Present State of the Hebrides and Western Coasts of Scotland* (Edinburgh, 1786, pirated edition printed in Dublin, 1746)
ANSON, PETER F. *Scots Fisherfolk* (Edinburgh, 1950)
——. *Underground Catholicism in Scotland* (Montrose, 1970)
BEVERIDGE, ERSKINE. *North Uist: Its Archaeology and Topography* (Edinburgh, 1911)
BRETON, FREDERICK. *Heroine in Homespun* (1893)
BUCHANAN, DONALD. *Reflections of the Isle of Barra* (1943)
BUCHANAN, J. L. *Travels in the Western Hebrides from 1782 to 1790* (1793)
BUCHANAN, R. *In Hebrid Isles* (1883)
CAMERON, ALEXANDER. *Reliquiae Celtica* (Inverness, 1882)
CAMPBELL, J. F. *Popular Tales of the West Highlands* (Edinburgh, 1864)
CAMPBELL, J. L. *Bardachd Mhgr Ailein* (Edinburgh, 1965)
——. *Fr Allan MacDonald of Eriskay, 1859–1905* (Edinburgh, 1954)
——. *Fr Allan MacDonald, Priest, Poet and Folklorist* (Edinburgh, 1956)
——. *Gaelic Folksongs from the Isle of Barra* (with 12in records) (1950)
—— (ed). *Gaelic Words and Expressions from South Uist and Eriskay* (Dublin, 1958)
——. *Sia Sgialachdan* (six Gaelic stories from Uist and Barra) (Edinburgh, 1938)
—— (ed). *Stories from South Uist* (1961)
—— (ed). *Tales of Barra, Told by the Coddy* (Edinburgh, 1959)
—— (ed). *The Book of Barra* (1936)
——, and COLLINSON, F. *Hebridean Folksongs* (1969)
——, and HALL, T. *Strange Things* (1968)
CARMICHAEL, ALEXANDER. *Carmina Gadelica*, 6 vols (Edinburgh, 1928–71)

THE UISTS AND BARRA

——. *Grazing and Agrestic Customs of the Outer Hebrides* (Edinburgh, 1884)

COOPER, P. *The So-called Evictions from the MacDonald Estates* (Aberdeen, 1881)

CRAIG, K. C. *Orain Luaidh Mairi Nighean Aladair* (155 Waulking songs of South Uist) (Glasgow, 1938)

CUMMING, C. F. GORDON. *In the Hebrides* (1886)

DARLING, F. FRASER. *Natural History in the Highlands and Islands* (1947)

——. *West Highland Survey* (Oxford, 1955)

DAY, J. P. *Public Administration in the Highlands and Islands of Scotland* (1918)

DUCKWORTH, C. L. D. and LANGMUIR, G. E. *West Highland Steamers* (Prescot, 1935, reprinted 1967)

GIBLIN, C. *The Irish Franciscan Mission to Scotland, 1619–46* (Dublin, 1964)

GILLIES, A. *A Hebridean in Goethe's Weimar* (Oxford, 1969)

GOODRICH-FREER, A. *The Outer Isles* (1902)

GRANT, I. F. *Angus Og of the Isles* (Edinburgh, 1969)

GRAY, ROBERT. *The Birds of the West of Scotland, including the Outer Hebrides* (Glasgow, 1871)

HAMILTON, J. R. C. (ed). *The Iron Age in North Britain* (1967)

HARVIE-BROWN, J. A. and BUCKLEY, T. E. *Vertebrate Fauna of the Outer Hebrides* (Edinburgh, 1889)

HERON, ROBERT. *General View of the Natural Circumstances of the Hebudae or Hebrides* (Edinburgh, 1794)

KEDDIE, H. *The MacDonald Lass* (1895)

KENNEDY FRASER, M. *Songs of the Hebrides*, 4 vols

LANG, ANDREW. *Pickle the Spy* (1897)

——. *The Highlands of Scotland in 1750* (Edinburgh, 1898)

MACCULLOCH, John. *The Highlands and Western Isles of Scotland* (1824)

MACDONALD, A. and MACDONALD, A. *The Clan Donald*, 3 vols (Inverness 1896–1904)

MACDONALD, A. *Uist Bards* (Glasgow, 1894)

——. *The MacDonald Collection of Gaelic Poetry* (Inverness, 1911)

MACDONALD, FLORA. *The Autobiography of Flora MacDonald* (edited by her grand-daughter), 2 vols (Edinburgh, 1870)

MACDONALD, JAMES. *General View of the Agriculture of the Hebrides* (Edinburgh, 1811)

MACFARLANE, A. *Geographical Collection* (Edinburgh, 1907)

MACINTOSH, W. C. *A Holiday in North Uist* (1865)

192

MACKENZIE, ALEXANDER. *The History of the Highland Clearances* (Glasgow 1883 and 1946)
MACKENZIE, W. C. *History of the Outer Hebrides* (Paisley, 1903)
——. *The Highlands and Islands of Scotland* (Edinburgh, 1937, revised 1949)
MACKENZIE, COMPTON. *My Life and Times; Octave Seven (1931–38)* (1968)
MACLAUCHLAN, T. *Recent Highland Ejections (in the Uists) Considered* (Edinburgh, 1950)
MACCLELLAN, ANGUS. *The Furrow Behind Me* (1962)
MACLEOD, DONALD. *Gloomy Memories* (Glasgow, 1892)
MACLEOD, KENNETH. *Songs of the Hebrides* (1909)
MACMILLAN, SOMERLED (ed). *Sporan Dhomhnaill* (Gaelic Poems and Songs by Donald MacIntyre) (Edinburgh, 1968)
MACMILLAN, J. *Gaelic Songs of the Isles of the West*, 2 vols. Translations and stories by Patrick MacGlynn. Music arranged by F. W. Lewis (1929, 1930)
MACNEIL OF BARRA. *Castle in the Sea* (Glasgow)
——. *The Clan MacNeil* (New York, 1923)
MACRURY, E. *A Hebridean Parish* (Inverness, 1950)
MARTIN, MARTIN. *A Description of the Western Isles of Scotland* (London, 1716; Glasgow, 1884)
MATHESON, W. (ed). *The Songs of John MacCodrum* (Edinburgh, 1938)
MILLER, HUGH. *The Cruise of the Betsey; or, A Summer Ramble Among the Hebrides* (Edinburgh, 1858)
Miscellanea Scotica (Glasgow, 1818)
MUIR, T. S. *Characteristics of Old Church Architecture, etc, in the Mainland and Western Islands of Scotland* (Edinburgh, 1861)
MUNRO, NEIL. *Children of the Tempest*
MUNRO, R. W. (ed). *Munro's Western Isles of Scotland* (Edinburgh, 1961)
MURRAY, A. *Father Allan's Island* (New York, 1920)
NECKER DE SAUSSURE, L. A. *Voyage en Ecosse at Aux Iles Hebrides* (Geneva, 1821)
New Statistical Account for Scotland (Edinburgh, 1845)
O'DELL, A. C. and WALTON, K. *The Highlands and Islands of Scotland* (Edinburgh, 1952)
Old Statistical Account for Scotland (Edinburgh, 1794)
O LOCHLAINN, COLM. *Deoch-slainte nan Gillean* (Dublin, 1948)
PEEL, C. V. A. *Wild Sport in the Outer Hebrides* (1901)
PLACE, ROBIN. *Introduction to Archaeology* (1968)

BIBLIOGRAPHY

POCHIN-MOULD, D. D. C. *West-over-Sea* (Edinburgh, 1953)

REA, F. G. *A School in South Uist* (1964)

Registrum Magni Sigilli Regum Scotorum (Edinburgh, 1882–1914)

SCOTTISH MOUNTAINEERING CLUB, THE. *The Islands of Scotland* (Edinburgh, 1961)

SHAW, MARGARET FAY. *Folksongs and Folklore of South Uist* (1955)

SIMPSON, W. D. *Portrait of Skye and the Outer Hebrides* (1967)

SINCLAIR, COLIN. *Thatched Houses* (Edinburgh, 1953)

SWIRE, O. *The Outer Hebrides and their Legends* (Edinburgh, 1966)

STRAND, PAUL. *Tir a' Mhurain* (1962)

THOMPSON, FRANCIS. *Ghosts, Spirits and Spectres of Scotland* (Aberdeen, 1973)

———. *Harris Tweed* (Newton Abbot, 1969)

———. *St Kilda and Other Hebridean Outliers* (Newton Abbot, 1970)

WATSON, J. CARMICHAEL. *Gaelic Songs of Mary MacLeod* (Edinburgh, 1934 and 1965)

WEBSTER CENSUS. *Scottish Population Statistics*, Scottish History Society, 3rd Series, vol 43 (Edinburgh, 1952)

WILSON, JAMES. *A Voyage Round the Coasts of Scotland and the Isles* (Edinburgh, 1842)

ARTICLES

BALFOUR, J. H. and BABINGTON, C. C. 'Catalogue of the plants gathered in the Islands of North Uist, Harris and Lewis', *Edinburgh Botanical Society Trans*, I, iii (1841)

BEDFORD, DUCHESS OF. 'Some autumn bird notes from the Outer Hebrides', *Annals of Scottish Natural History*, XVIII (1909)

BLUNDELL, F. ODO. 'The State of the Catholic Religion in the Hebrides in 1671', *Catholic Quarterly Review*, XXXVI (1911)

BORGSTROM, CARL HJ. 'The Dialect of Barra in the Outer Hebrides', *Norsk Tidsskrift for Sprogvidenskap*, Bins VIII (Oslo, 1935)

CAIRD, J. B. 'The Human Geography of the Outer Hebrides', *Scottish Geographical Magazine*, vol 74 (1958)

———, and MOISLEY, H. A. 'Leadership and Innovation in the Crofting Communities of the Outer Hebrides', *The Sociological Review*, vol 9, no 1 (1961)

CAMPBELL, J. L. 'Eviction at First Hand', *The Scots Magazine* (January 1945)

———. 'Fr Allan MacDonald, Miss A. Goodrich Freer, and Hebridean Folklore', *Scottish Studies*, vol II

——. 'The Macro Lepidoptera of the Parish of Barra', *Scot Naturalist*, no 234 (1938)

——. 'Migrant Lepidoptera in Barra', *Scot Naturalist* (1936)

——. 'Proverbs from Barra', *Scottish Gaelic Studies*, vol X, pt II (1965)

——, and EASTWICK, C. 'The MacNeils of Barra in the Forty-five', *The Innes Review*, vol XVII

CRAWFORD, I. A. 'Contributions to a History of Domestic Settlement in North Uist', *Scottish Studies*, vol 9, pt 1 (1965)

DAVIES, G. L. 'The Parish of North Uist', *Scot Geographical Magazine*, vol 72 (1958)

FORREST, J. E., WATERSTON, A. R. and WATSON, E. V. 'The Natural History of Barra, Outer Hebrides', *Proc Roy Physical Soc, Edinburgh*, vol XXII (1936)

GEDDES, A. 'Land Utilisation in the Highlands and the Western Isles', *Scot Geographical Magazine*, vol 51 (1945)

GOODRICH-FREER, A. 'Eriskay and Prince Charlie', *Blackwoods Magazine*, vol CLXIX (1901)

GRAY, M. 'The Kelp Industry in the Highlands and Islands', *Economic History Review*, 2nd series, IV, no 2 (1951)

HARRISON, J. W. HESLOP. 'A Contribution to our knowledge of the Lepidoptera of the Islands of Coll, Canna, Sanday, Rhum, Eigg, Soay and Pabbay (Inner Hebrides) and of Barra, Mingulay and Berneray (Outer Hebrides)', *Proc Univ Durham Phil Soc*, vol XI (1938)

HOBSON, P. M. 'The Parish of Barra', *Scot Geographical Magazine*, vol 65 (1949)

KINNEAR, N. B. 'Notes on the Birds seen in the Outer Hebrides during the Spring of 1906', *Annals Scot Natural Hist* (1907)

LETHBRIDGE, T. C. 'Excavations at Kilphedar', *Proc Prehistory Soc*, New Series, 18 (1952)

MACKAY, IAN. 'Clanranald's Tacksmen', *Trans Gaelic Soc Inverness*, vol XLIV (1964–6)

MACKIE, E. W. 'Brochs and the Hebridean Iron Age', *Antiquity*, XXXIX (1965)

——. 'The Origin and Development of the Broch and Wheelhouse Building Cultures of the Scottish Iron Age', *Proc Prehistory Soc*, vol XXXI (1965)

MACLAREN, A. 'Viking House at Drimore', *Discovery and Excavation* (1956)

MARWICK, T. 'Notes on the Mammals of the Isles of Barra, Mingulay and Berneray, Outer Hebrides', *The Scottish Naturalist*, no 230 (1938)

MILLER, R. 'Land Use by Summer Shielings', *Scottish Studies*, vol 11, pt 2 (1967)

MOISLEY, H. A. 'The Deserted Hebrides', *Scottish Studies*, vol 10, pt 1 (1966)

——. 'North Uist in 1799', *Scot Geographical Magazine*, vol 83 (1967)

MURCHISON, T. M. 'Deserted Hebridean Isles', *Trans Gaelic Soc Inverness*, vol XLII (1953–9)

RANKING, D. F. 'Barra—Past and Present', *Celtic Monthly*, vol XII (1904)

RITCHIE, W. 'The Machair of South Uist', *Scot Geographical Magazine*, vol 83 (1967)

——. 'The Post-glacial rise in sea level and coastal changes in the Uists', *Trans Inst British Geography* (1966)

SCOTT, L. 'Gallo-British Colonies: the Aisled Round-house Culture in the North', *Proc Prehistory Soc*, vol XIV (1948)

SHAW, M. F. 'Hunting Folksongs in the Hebrides', *Nat Geographic Magazine* (February 1947)

SINCLAIR, A. M. 'The MacNeils of Barra', *Celtic Review*, vol III

WEDDERSPOON, J. 'Shell Middens of the Outer Hebrides', *Trans Inverness Field Club*, vol VIII (1906–12)

YOUNG, A. and RICHARDSON, J. M. ' "A" Cheardach Mhor, Drimore, South Uist', *Proc Soc Antiquaries of Scotland*, vol XCIII (1959)

MISCELLANEOUS REPORTS, PAPERS, MSS, ETC

ANDERSON, J. *An Account of the Present State of the Hebrides* (Report to the Lords of the Treasury, 1785)

Balranald Papers MS (1764). Unpublished Balranald Estate Papers of 1764 in private hands

Census, 1961, Scotland, vol 7, Gaelic (HMSO, 1966)

Census, 1966, Sample, Scotland, County Report (HMSO, 1967)

Clanranald Papers, Factors Reports and Additional Clanranald Papers (Scottish Records Office)

CRAIG, J. C. *South Uist Gaelic*, Thesis No 1344 (1955). University of Glasgow

CROFTERS COMMISSION. Minutes of Evidence taken by HM Commissioners of inquiry into the condition of the crofters and cottars in the Highlands and Islands of Scotland (Parl Paper), 5 vols (Edinburgh, 1884)

———. Annual Reports (Inverness). In progress

HIGHLANDS & ISLANDS DEVELOPMENT BOARD. *Annual Reports* (Inverness). In progress

HIGHLAND TRANSPORT BOARD. *Highland Transport Services* (HMSO, 1967)

JUSTICIARY RECORDS. Books of Adjornal, 3 June 1678 and 4 July 1682

MACDONALD, A. (Killearnan). MS *History in 'The Carmichael Papers' in Edinburgh University Library*

MACDONALD, A. J. (Sydney, Australia). MS of *North Uist Traditions* (copies deposited in the School of Scottish Studies, Edinburgh; Celtic Dept, Glasgow University; and Paible JS School, N. Uist)

NICOLSON, ALEXANDER. *Report on the State of Education in the Hebrides* (Education Commission, Scotland; Edinburgh, 1866)

REID, ROBERT. MS *Plan of the Island of North Uist* (1799) (Register House Plan no 1306)

RITCHIE, W. *The Coastal Geomorphology of North Uist*, O'Dell Monograph no 1 (Dept of Geography, University of Aberdeen, 1968)

ROYAL COMMISSION ON AGRICULTURE. Reports (1879)

SCOTT, W. R. *Report to the Board of Agriculture for Scotland on Home Industries in the Highlands and Islands* (Parl Paper) (Edinburgh, 1914)

SCOTTISH HOME & HEALTH DEPARTMENT. *General Medical Services in the Highlands and Islands* (Report of a Committee, Edinburgh, 1967)

SCOTS COLLEGE, ROME. Letters written from South Uist, Barra and Vatersay to Rev Angus MacDonald, Rector of the Scots College at Rome, between 4 February 1827 and 4 March 1831

SOCIETY FOR THE SUPPORT OF GAELIC SCHOOLS. Reports (Edinburgh, 1811–45)

SSPCK. Minutes; deposited in Register House, Edinburgh

WESTERN ISLES TOURIST ASSOCIATION. *Official Guide* (Stornoway, various dates)

AUTHOR'S NOTE

WORKING within the confines of an imposed word limit it has been necessary to compress a large mass of detail into a picture of these islands which is, it is readily granted, brief; but the author hopes that it is adequate. To enable readers to obtain fuller information on most of the important aspects of the islands a comprehensive bibliography has been given.

I am more than grateful for the help which a large number of people offered me during the preparation of this book. They are too numerous to mention by name; I trust the book itself will serve as a suitable witness and reminder of their willing co-operation in the production of facts, figures and snippets of useful information which have all added to make the book, the author hopes, a definitive work on these islands.

In particular I express thanks to Dr John L. Campbell, of Canna, for much useful information of typically excellent quality; I. R. MacKay, Inverness, for guidance in the presentation of vital social and cultural aspects of South Uist and Barra; and Dr Kenneth Robertson, Daliburgh, for his excellent pictures which record contemporary life in these islands. I wish also to record my appreciation of the interest taken by the late Sir Compton MacKenzie, particularly regarding the Sea League of Barra.

I owe thanks, too, to the *Stornoway Gazette*, for making its valuable files accessible to me at various times for research on island subjects covering half a century; and to the facilities of the Library of the Gaelic Society of Inverness, wherein is deposited much information on the past history of the Outer Hebrides.

I take this final opportunity of thanking my wife, Margaret, for her wonderful forbearance during the long periods of research, assimilation and final writing of this book, and its companions in the 'Islands' Series of my publishers, which have amounted to many months while her husband worked in the isolation of his study. *Moran taing dhuibhse uile.*

INDEX

Italic numerals indicate illustration pages

INDEX